© 2026 by Greg Hawks & Hawks Media
All rights reserved.

Thank you for purchasing an authorized edition of this book and for complying with copyright law. No part of this book may be reproduced, stored in a retrieval system, or transmitted by any means, electronic, mechanical, photocopying, recording, or otherwise, without prior written permission from the copyright holder.

For ordering information or special discounts for bulk purchases, please contact: hello@greghawks.com | 405-393-0990

ISBN: 979-8-9931784-0-0
Library of Congress Control Number: 2025920475

Cover design: Monica Sheri Scott
Interior design: Monica Sheri Scott & Greg Hawks

This is a work of nonfiction. Some names and identifying details have been changed to protect the privacy of individuals.

First Edition, 2026
Printed in the United States of America.

10 9 8 7 6 5 4 3 2 1

HAWKS MEDIA
Minneapolis, MN

Dedicated to my Mom.

CONTENTS

Foreword — IX
Origin Story — XII

Part 1: Building the Ownership Metaphor

Introduction: The Engagement Deficit — 1
Chapter 1: Vandals Bring Division and Strife — 9
Chapter 2: Renters Bring Only Their Hands — 19
Chapter 3: Owners Bring Their Heart, Head, and Hands — 29

Part 2: The Five Unlocks of an Owner's Mindset

Chapter 4: It Goes Both Ways — 39
Chapter 5: Risk Bold Commitments — 47
Chapter 6: Activate Lasting Value — 67
Chapter 7: Reach for Responsibility — 83
Chapter 8: Widen the Circle — 99
Chapter 9: Think Whole House — 109
Chapter 10: Your Life Is An Investment — 119

Part 3: Creating a Culture of Ownership

Chapter 11:	Lease-Purchase Option	135
Chapter 12:	The Loyalty Dilemma	151
Chapter 13:	Designing an Ownership Culture	159
Chapter 14:	Conclusion	173

Beyond the Book

Case Study:	A 10-Year Culture Journey	179
Bibliography		193
Acknowledgments		201
Personal Note		203
About the Author		205

FOREWORD

When HoganTaylor took the big leap to function as a unified business, the partners voted me to be the firm's first full-time CEO and Chairman of the newly established Board of Directors. This was a big change for our firm. Alongside our great hopes and expectations there was much uncertainty. In my new role, I had so many questions.

What is it that we are actually trying to accomplish? What do we believe most? What are our main values? Where are we going? What is our vision?

I needed to understand what we really valued and how we should agree to interact with each other to become something more, better, and greater.

Greg Hawks and his emphasis on ownership culture and core values answered my need. Greg helped us define and implement our aspirational values that would create our culture and give depth to our mission. He accomplished this through a high energy, challenging, and motivational process that involved scores of people over a few months.

I remember focus groups of our people answering hard questions about what we were doing right and where we needed to improve. I was grateful for a lot, shocked by some, and humbled by it all. The process required a leader who had strong social skills and managerial courage, someone who valued the purpose behind the project so much they would not allow shortcuts. Greg provided all of that for us. What came of that process is what we call HT3, our core set of values. HT3 defines our aspirations, gives depth to our behaviors, and guides how we recruit, evaluate performance, and make promotions. Created over 14 years ago, HT3 has stood the test of every hard thing the market has thrown at us. It is in our DNA.

Our firm has been involved in many merger acquisitions over the years whereby we have increased market share, expanded to new geographies, and added new service lines. A consistent theme through all these events is how we promote who we are and what we value most. HT3 not only centers the firm on who

FOREWORD

we are and hope to become, but serves to attract other like-minded individuals and organizations to us.

When it comes to culture and promoting our values in alignment with our strategic plan, no other day on the annual calendar is more important than our firm meeting day. For 14 years straight Greg has served as a leader alongside our creative team in the months-long process of developing a theme, organizing our activities, and serving as the Emcee for a full day of high energy purpose and joy. Our firm meetings are strategic in focus, creative, celebratory, and loads of fun. Greg works tirelessly with our creative team to plan and execute each event to deepen our ownership of our values and strategic imperatives. He is funny and engaging, but always strategic and focused. With Greg's involvement and visibility in these annual events, it is clear he takes his ownership message and principles to heart, living by them as an example to those he serves.

One note on the creativity of our firm meetings. Greg has an endless supply of ideas no matter the topic. It is not unusual for some sort of "dress in character" to be part of the fun. As our Emcee, Greg jumps right in and leads the way in wearing costumes or uniforms to support our theme. This is one more example of his commitment to making our firm meetings the best they can be. Yes, he is a highly skilled motivational speaker, but you should see him dressed up as the Rabbit in our Alice-In-Wonderland-themed meeting.

I have not come across a partner in cultural development, or any consultant for that matter, who has more energy to engage and inspire a group of people to become their best selves. Greg believes in helping people and wants to see his clients succeed. He pours his heart and soul into the process that he uses with clients. This process embodies the principles outlined in this book.

Because every organization is different, the words that we use to define our culture, beliefs, and behaviors are not the specific words you will read in this book; however, Greg's underlying principles are foundational to what we have built and continue to build. I imagine they will become foundational for you as well. You can trust Greg and the ideas in this book to help your organization answer the question "Who Owns This Place?" and then move people towards acting like owners.

Randy Nail
Chief Executive Officer HoganTaylor
Top 100 Accounting + Advisory Firm

ORIGIN **STORY**

I opened the front door of the second house I'd ever bought as an investment property, eager to prepare it for new tenants after my first tenants, a group of college guys, moved out. A putrid stench assaulted my nostrils. It was the smell of wet clothes unlaundered for months, beer and soda permanently embedded in the carpet, old food left out, and months of sweat that had rubbed everywhere.

I walked through the four-bedroom home, horrified, feeling like I might not be able to keep my lunch down. Each room could have been a crime scene exhibit. In one room the wall was concave, as if some big football player had been tackled into it. Another room had holes all over the walls. Apparently an angry kid had taken his aggression out on the drywall. Weirdly another room had inexplicable stains in odd places.

The new carpet I'd been proud to install just before they moved in was completely destroyed. Beer, soda, food, dirt, grease, and who knows what else was ground into the fabric. I'd chosen a light brown carpet with flecks of darker brown to help hide wear and tear. These stains were too colorful, too dark, and too huge to be hidden.

In room after room, there was random destruction, including broken windowpanes, toilets cracked or loosened from the floor, tubs and showers full of mold, ripped linoleum, broken cabinet doors, missing knobs, broken ceiling fans, and leaky faucets. It was as if someone intentionally went into each room to see how many things they could break. Not a room was left unscathed. The devastation cost thousands of dollars to repair and left my soul drained. I questioned my ability and willingness to continue pursuing my investment property dream. It's an odd sensation to be emotionally crushed by strangers and an inanimate object. But there I was, in tears.

Afterwards, I spoke with the students and their parents to determine who was responsible. I've never seen the blame game played so perfectly. To each parent, their child was an angel and the rest were devils. Each student claimed it was the other three boys, and their friends, who were the culprits. Blame, blame, blame; justify, justify, justify; this is the language of vandals. While they rationalize how nothing is ever their fault, they engage in destructive activity that will cost you dearly.

At the time, I was the Executive Director of a non-profit that worked with teenagers. I had a small full-time staff. We also hired summer staff and interns. There were literally hundreds of volunteers who worked with us every summer to run camps that slept 840 kids and leaders a week. We programmed 18-hour days. Monday through Thursday, from 6am until 1am, we were working. On Friday, they left by noon and our teams were asleep by 12:05. (Just kidding. They worked extraordinarily hard to turn the place around and get it ready for the next weeks' group of students.) I loved my job and the people I worked with.

After the vandal house, the parallels between my investment property life and my leadership life started to crystalize. I noticed amongst the different staffers, some of them truly owned their responsibilities and supported the camper experience. Others seemed to simply do the minimum necessary. A few even undermined our mission.

It all came into focus for me. Some of my team were *owners*. Some of them were *renters*. And a few of them were *vandals*.

ACT LIKE AN OWNER

For a decade as Executive Director, I worked with hundreds of people and served tens of thousands of campers. My philosophy came into shape across those years. I realized both renters and owners had a role to play in fulfilling our mission. But vandals, I needed to evict them as quickly as possible.

The position, job description, and pay were not what determined if a person took on an owner, renter, or vandal role. I had a guy, let's call him Steve, who worked security at the campground gate for years. He literally sat in a chair in 100+ degree Oklahoma heat starting out. He quickly got us a tent set up. Then he figured out how to run electricity to this desolate location. Eventually, we built a gatehouse, primarily because one volunteer was passionate about serving and creating a place others could serve, too. Security Gate Steve *owned* that role ... as a volunteer. He frequently took vacation days from his real job to serve at camp. Also, he randomly worked the overnight shift. The guy cared deeply!

I had other people who were paid and didn't bring that much passion or imagination to their role. They showed up on time, did their job, then went home. They didn't create issues. They weren't destructive or divisive. Their contribution was their skill. I had people on stage who were talented and gifted, but didn't own their role. They performed their job and did fine, but that's where their contribution ended. They were *renters*.

And finally, every camp season I'd get a few folks who became disenchanted with reality and complained about the limitations of our resources. They tended to think the area they had responsibilities in were being overlooked and thought leadership was always wrong. They took their complaints and perspectives sideways and downward. On some occasions they'd infect others with this virus of negativity and division. They'd even go so far as to quietly, but purposely, sabotage our efforts. They prioritized themselves over the other staff and campers and were detrimental to the mission of the organization. While they didn't cause property damage, like those college guys, they were vandals, too! Their destruction was subtle, but painful. Some of them had to be fired or sent home.

Vandals are not restricted to summer camps. There are vandals in many workplaces. They may not always destroy property, but they work directly against the vision of the company. They are divisive, arrogant, and self-centered. They are gossipers, silent saboteurs, and active dissenters. They resist real progress while promoting their own accomplishments. They quietly suggest that leadership's vision will never happen while abstaining from trying to make it a reality. They don't contribute to the collective efforts. Some of them think and feel superior, while others live in cynicism, resentment, disappointment, or anger.

Every organization has renters, too. They know what needs to be done. They know how to do it. They work consistently and reliably. However, they possess what I call a *renter's mindset*. People with a renter's mindset may enjoy their work, but they've concluded it's not worth the effort to go all in with their full hearts and minds. They do what's expected, and no more. Sometimes they move casually between companies, seeing each one as the next step for their immediate needs, without buying into the company's culture and mission.

People have a renter's mindset, literally or figuratively, for a variety of reasons. However, there is an opportunity for greater investment, engagement, and return. I've had tenants who've planted gardens, re-dug the flower beds, put up fences, added stones, and made many other improvements. Though they were renting, they possessed an *owner's mindset*. People with an owner's mindset, like Security Gate Steve, invest their hearts and heads in the home even when they don't actually own it. They care about the place because they and their family live there. They find fulfillment in treating it like they own it, since it's where they're building their life at this time.

There are people in many workplaces who do the same thing.

ORIGIN STORY

They care. A lot. About their work, their colleagues, their clients, and their organization. They care about results, process, accuracy, excellence, and many other qualities that give them satisfaction about what they've achieved. They use their imagination, are open to new ideas, engage in challenging conversations, and remain flexible. Workplaces thrive when they are filled with people who have an owner's mindset!

Understanding these three mindsets—*vandal*, *renter*, *owner*—gives us greater insight into our colleagues, leaders, direct reports, and ourselves. It's not like a DiSC personality assessment or Meyers-Briggs type, but once we identify how we're approaching our personal and professional lives, it clarifies why we're getting what we're getting in life. What's wild is that we can bring an ownership mindset to one area of life, while thinking like a renter in another, and heaven forbid, exhibit vandal tendencies in yet another. It's not an either/or proposition. By understanding these mindsets, we can promote acting like an owner in ourselves and others, and also promote an ownership culture in our organization.

Time and time again, when I talk about the mindsets of *vandals*, *renters*, and *owners*, audiences and clients resonate with these concepts because of how accurately they illuminate reality. I've given hundreds of keynotes, worked with numerous businesses, government agencies, big companies, non-profits, universities, associations, and other organizations, while also doing some deep culture work with a variety of cool clients. You'll hear about a few of them throughout these pages. What I hear consistently is that this framework is easily relatable, immediately useful, and everyone gets it. I hope this is the case for you. When I return to clients for a second or third time, they share specific stories about how this message has improved the culture of their companies. They expand the metaphor in ways that I hadn't considered. Please feel free to do the same.

I had the opportunity to work with the leadership team at DHEC, a 100% employee-owned electrical and telecom contracting firm. During our time together, I heard story after story of team members taking initiative, collaborating across departments, and treating the business like it was their own—so much so that employees launched four other business units that now make up the "Davis H. Elliot Family of Brands." How did a company that ran power lines overhead and buried fiber optics get into the video production business? Or start a fractional IT company?

Simple. DHEC created an environment of listening and enabling their people to unlock potential in unconventional ways. They fostered an ownership culture that wasn't limited to the task at hand. They promoted a place for the employee-owners to consider how they could make the organization more valuable and more effective. It's built into how they hire, train, and lead. What's fascinating is that their success is not because they have an ESOP (Employee Stock Ownership Plan), but because they've created a space where ideas are welcome and broad thinking is supported. This all existed before I spent time with them. I simply got to build upon their decades of success.

Speaking of success, I did fix the vandalized house. It took quite an investment, but I made everything right again. I also went on to buy ten more homes after it. So it didn't stifle me too much. However, in a very random coincidence, no college guys ever lived in any of my properties again. I don't recall if they didn't apply or weren't approved.

In this book, I share what I have learned from my decades in real estate, consulting, speaking, and leading a non-profit. We'll discover how we can think and act like an owner as well as cultivate an ownership culture at work. I'm grateful you are reading. I'm confident this book has the capacity to generate new language and new ways of thinking. My hope is that leaders and teams will utilize it as a blueprint to create work, life, and cultures that produces fulfillment and impact.

PART 1

BUILDING THE OWNERSHIP METAPHOR

INTRODUCTION
THE ENGAGEMENT DEFICIT

Think about the last time your favorite team won a championship. Maybe it was your alma mater. Maybe it was your city's underdog franchise finally pulling it off. (*I just got this experience when the OKC Thunder won the NBA Championship Title!*) Possibly your team has been on a winning streak. Or maybe it was a team you didn't even care about, but the story pulled you in. Their energy. The grit. How they played for, and with, each other.

What made that team great?

Some teams are close-knit, a band of sisters or brothers. Others are competitive and argumentative, a squad of rivals.

They may dominate with flash and talent, win through team chemistry, or grind their way to victory. Whatever the style, there's always one thing you'll see in championship teams.

EVERYONE IS ENGAGED!

No one's checked out. No one's dragging the team down or undermining others' efforts. Whatever their disagreements or differing approaches, everyone is there to win!

Every person is in the game, even if on the sideline.

Think about your current or past workplaces. Have you encountered that level of investment? Every leader, manager, and employee locked in like that? Fully engaged. Personally invested. Willing to give their best, not just for the paycheck, but for the people around them and the mission they're trying to accomplish.

Sound like a fantasy? An unachievable utopia? Let's be honest (and I always will be), most teams don't look or feel like that. Not even close.

Gallup has been tracking workplace engagement for 25 years. And the results have stayed ... mostly consistent.

On average over the last 25 years 31% of people are engaged, 52% are disengaged, and 17% are actively disengaged.

THE ENGAGEMENT DEFICIT

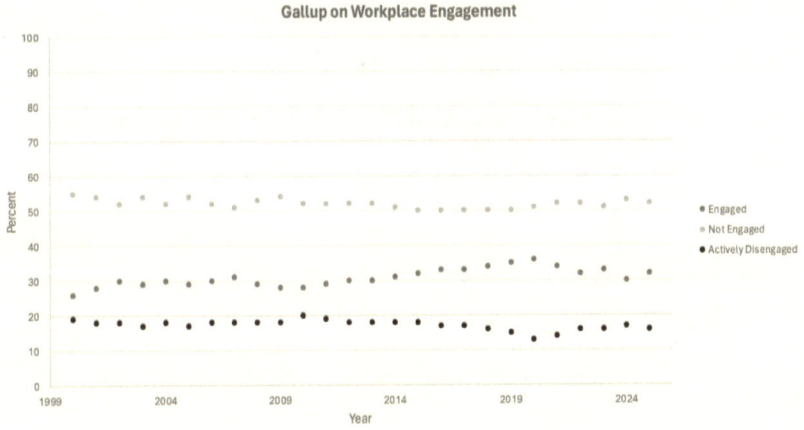

Teams with that profile never win championships. They remain average. What would it be like if your company had the engagement level of a championship team? For most of us, even a little progress towards that goal would make a major impact on the quality of our work, the joy of our environment, and the performance of our organization.

Everyone wants employee engagement increased. We take surveys, create initiatives, and implement strategies, yet produce the same results year after year. It's frustrating. It's a hard thing to alter, as Gallup's 25 years' worth of data reveals.

How do we shift buy-in from a desperate wish into a legitimate result?

We anchor it in metaphor.

The ownership metaphor provides a simple but powerful lens for reimagining how people show up to work (and life). Taking Gallup's abstract categories and turning them into actionable realities, enables almost everyone to retain it:

- The 31% of employees who are engaged? Owners.
- The 52% who are disengaged? Renters.
- And the 17% who are actively disengaged? Vandals.

My shorthand descriptor for each is...

OWNERS BRING THEIR HEART, HEAD, AND HANDS.
RENTERS BRING ONLY THEIR HANDS.
VANDALS BRING DIVISION AND STRIFE.

WHY THE METAPHOR WORKS

The word "engagement" is fuzzy. It's a well-meaning term, but also a moving target. Does engagement mean long hours? Constant activity? Inbox zero?

If you've got kids, adult-care responsibilities, or value life outside of work, you'll resist that kind of definition before the conversation even starts. And if your calendar is packed but your heart's checked out, does that mean you are engaged?

THE ENGAGEMENT DEFICIT

ENGAGED = OWNERS
HEART + HEAD + HANDS

 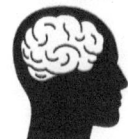 

DISENGAGED = RENTERS
HANDS

ACTIVELY DISENGAGED = VANDALS
DIVISION + STRIFE

Probably not.

Depending on your Generation Label (X,Y, Z or Boomer), you also have a different relationship with engagement. Granted "ownership" can be elusive, as well. I hope you'll find alignment as you continue to read.

That's why asking people to be "more engaged" is ineffective. It's like telling someone to "care more." Inspiring, maybe … but unhelpful.

We all know the pride of making something we *own*. We also know the temptation to disengage when it's "not our problem." And you and I certainly know what it's like to clean up after someone who doesn't care.

This isn't about squeezing more from people. It's about inviting others into a deeper sense of identity, connection, and contribution. It makes engagement *real* and the path to incorporating it *possible*. I'm offering objectivity to the subjective idea of owning your role and being someone who is "bought in."

It turns out this isn't just a communication hack, but neuroscience. According to Chip and Dan Heath in *Made to Stick* (Heath and Heath 2007), metaphors help people grasp complex or abstract ideas by connecting them to something concrete and familiar. When I say someone's "renting their role" or "acting like a vandal," we don't need a slide deck. Everyone gets it.

That's why in Part 1, we'll dive deep into the metaphor itself, through the lens of both real estate and the workplace. You'll meet owners, renters, and vandals in their natural habitats. You'll begin to see how these mindsets operate within the culture of your organization.

In Part 2 we'll explore the Unlocks. Have you ever played a video game and wanted to get to the NEXT LEVEL? How did you unlock that level? You acquired skills, abilities, strategies, resources, and experience to reach it. The Five Unlocks are the central piece of this book. Applying yourself diligently to them will give you a new experience in life and at work. The Unlocks are mindshifts that enable you to see the world and your work from a new perspective.

In Part 3, we'll take a macro view on workplace culture, loyalty, and what it takes to invite someone to buy back in. People start out the first day on the job with an ownership mindset. We'll see how over the course of time, the work culture can turn them into renters. Asking someone to act like an owner again is possible, but requires a thoughtful approach. By the end, you'll have actionable ideas for how to build an ownership culture in your organization.

CHAPTER 1
VANDALS BRING DIVISION AND STRIFE

In 2001, after closing on the first home I ever bought as an investment property, I rolled up my sleeves and got to work. Cleaned it up. Swapped out faucets. Painted a few bedrooms. Then I planted a "For Rent" sign in the front yard and listed it on Craigslist. I was *fired up*. This was the beginning of my empire-building side hustle.

What I didn't expect was how many people would say they were coming and never show. Or how many were in really tough situations. Or how many would try some shady financial finagling. ("I'll give you $200 cash right now if I can have it.")

The excitement started to fade when I realized just how hard it was to find a good tenant.

Eventually, a single guy named Mike rented the home. That sparked my enthusiasm again. I figured, "One guy? What could go wrong?" Maybe he won't even use some of the rooms." For a few months, everything was hunky-dory. Mike paid rent. We didn't talk. Life moved on.

Until month five. No rent check appeared. That was unusual. I called Mike. No answer. That was more unusual.

A couple days later, I stopped by and knocked on the door. Nothing. Now I was getting nervous. My heart started racing. "What if Mike died in the house?! That's going to make it hard to rent." I walked around and looked in the windows. Mike's furniture was still there. His computer was there. But no Mike.

I started calling daily. Still nothing. I wasn't sure if I could legally go inside, but eventually I did. It was just like I'd seen from the windows. Everything was in place, except his clothes were gone. It was creepy. Like Mike had just vanished.

At that point, I decided I'd sell everything inside to help recover the unpaid rent and move on. Plot twist. *Mike didn't own any of it.* He'd been renting the furniture. The fridge. Even the computer. I had to call the police, post legal notices, and wait through a long, annoying process to reclaim *my own house* from a guy who ghosted me.

That's when I realized Mike was a vandal. Not the make-holes-in-the-walls kind. He abandoned his responsibility. Didn't tell me. Didn't return anything. Left me to chase down companies so I could give them their stuff back. It was annoying. I'd never even considered it a risk that a grown adult would just walk away from his commitment.

I never found out what happened to Mike.

Do you know someone like Mike at work? People with no attachment to the company who are willing to leave people in the lurch. They may not even exit the building, but rather do the minimum, abdicating responsibilities so others are forced to take up their slack. They don't care how much other people are affected or the negative impact it has on the company.

There was a season a few years back where people were "quiet quitting." They didn't leave their job, they just stopped doing the work. Oh, they still took the paycheck. Physically present, but mentally and emotionally vacated from the property. They justified their inaction by blaming the company or boss. It had a rebel feel to it, but it was vandal behavior. Somebody eventually had to do the work they weren't doing.

Vandals have a "ME FIRST" mindset. They can't be bothered with how their actions, or inaction, affect others. Sometimes they're subtle and other times overt. Consistently inconsiderate. Unintentionally disregarding. Typically oblivious.

> **VANDALS HAVE A "ME FIRST" MINDSET**

Vandals are the opposite of a team player. They think they're the star of the show and everyone else should be grateful they're carrying such a load.

Vandals are both a morale and economic issue. According to Gallup, actively disengaged employees cost companies worldwide $483 billion annually in lost productivity, absenteeism, turnover, and poor quality of work (Gallup 2023). Vandals drain teams, leaders, and resources, slowly eroding the environment from the inside out.

When I collaborate with an organization, I get a lot of access to leaders and teams. On one such occasion I spoke with an individual who was resisting a change that leadership was trying to make. He had worked there several years and had fallen into the trap of thinking "*I've seen this before. It's not going to work.*" His past experiences with the previous leadership informed his attitude toward their current initiative.

VANDALS BRING DIVISION AND STRIFE

Unlike the college guys from the introduction who actively destroyed, these vandals silently and insidiously corrode. While the physical destruction of property is seen, the quiet undercutting of leadership and working against forward progress is felt. Patching a hole in the wall is easier than defusing a subtle mutiny or rebuilding broken trust.

Gossip is a tool of vandals. I've worked with many companies where the fastest way to disseminate information is to put it in the form of gossip. Using fabricated, half-true, or even true stories to discredit, discourage, sow dissent, or rally the discouraged is a centuries-old maneuver. Speaking about the decisions leadership makes, while having a "behind-the-scenes" story that creates an entirely different narrative, is not uncommon. I'd share specific examples, but then it might sound like I'm gossiping too.

SIGNS OF A VANDAL

- SILENT SABOTEUR
- OBSTRUCTOR
- CONDESCENDING
- TOXIC TEAMMATE
- MOMENTUM KILLER
- SELFISH
- BLAMER
- GOSSIPER
- QUIET RESISTER
- PROGRESS BLOCKER

ACT LIKE AN OWNER

Why would anyone let a vandal live in their house? Why do organizations let almost 20% of their workforce act like vandals? I've discovered four reasons vandals remain.

1. They are **revenue generators**. They provide a disproportionate amount of significant financial impact to the organization and therefore tend to disregard others with impunity.
2. They have been on the team **a long time**. People say about these characters "they only have two or three more years until they retire." They do and say things that are not appropriate, but they've never been addressed about it before, so leadership crosses their fingers hoping no one files a lawsuit.
3. They are **related** to someone in authority. There are many upsides working with family. There are also some downsides. Sometimes, with blood relatives, an invisible shield is applied. Like an ambassador from another country, they are immune from consequences. And they know it.
4. They are the **owner** of the company. I know this seems wildly counterproductive, but sometimes an owner (or C-suite leader) can think "I was here before any of you. I did this without you. If you don't like it, you can hit the road." This one is so unfortunate because often they don't realize the destructive nature of their words.

Adam Neumann, co-founder and former CEO of WeWork, is a vivid example of a modern corporate vandal (Campbell 2023). On the outside, he was celebrated as a visionary, but inside the company, his leadership unraveled into chaos fueled by impulsive decisions, lavish spending, and emotional unpredictability. He hired based on loyalty rather than competence, punished dissent, and micromanaged his inner circle. Employees described a toxic environment where fear replaced trust and decisions were driven by ego, not strategy.

Neumann manipulated WeWork's culture for his own benefit. That's what vandals do. They don't just step back from responsibility, they use their influence to erode the trust, clarity, and cohesion that others are trying to build. Eventually, the cracks in the culture caught up. WeWork's IPO collapsed. Neumann was forced to step down. He left a broken business model and a broken culture.

My primary philosophy is to arrest and evict vandals. Get them out as soon as possible. It's difficult because they often contribute in ways that are both critical and significant. However, as Malcolm Gladwell confirms in *Revenge of the Tipping Point* (2024), one percentage point makes a huge difference. When you decrease the number of vandals, it has an exponential impact on the willingness of those with a renter's mindset to consider acting like an owner again. We don't realize re-engaging hearts and heads isn't always about the person themselves. Frequently people observe what leaders tolerate from a vandal and conclude there is no reason for them to invest themselves because of the inequality.

If the number of vandals decrease, it's almost certain the number of owners will increase. If you're in a place of leadership, put this to the test. If you are not in leadership, I suspect you have been frustrated and disappointed because vandals are roaming your halls and it seems no one is doing anything about it. A few tips to consider:

1. Raise concerns directly and consistently. Bring specific issues to your supervisor with clarity and professionalism rather than letting frustration fester.
2. Avoid fueling negativity. Resist the urge to vent or gossip with colleagues; it only spreads the very behavior you're hoping to reduce.
3. Recognize leadership's broader challenges. Extend measured grace to your leaders, knowing they may be balancing complexities or constraints you don't see.
4. Communicate the personal impact. Express how a vandal's behavior is affecting your work, your team, and the culture.

VANDALS BRING DIVISION AND STRIFE

For every percentage point vandal influence goes up, the effect is exponentially negative (Housman and Minor 2015). It can be hard to notice right away because they can be the stars producing results. Uber experienced such a scenario (Fisher 2024). During their hypergrowth phase, a few brilliant engineers became untouchable. They were known for delivering big. They crushed deadlines and wrote slick code. But they were also dismissive, territorial, and impossible to work with. They refused to document their systems. Wouldn't do code reviews. Mocked less experienced engineers. Hoarded knowledge like it was currency. And leadership let it ride. Why? Because these "brilliant jerks" (Fisher 2024) got results. Meanwhile, morale tanked, collaboration died, and a quiet resentment spread through the team like mold in the walls. No one smashed the servers or stormed out. They didn't need to. That's the thing about vandals, they don't have to break the product to break the people.

WHAT DO LEADERS TOLERATE

To destroy a culture, all you need is enough people who care more about themselves than the mission. Vandals come in many forms, from checked-out quiet quitters to gossiping pot-stirrers to high-performers who leave emotional bruises wherever they go. If you're in leadership, your silence can signal approval. And if you're not, your tolerance still shapes the environment. Our responsibility is to hold the standard. When the influence of vandals is reduced, we open the door for renters to re-engage and act like owners.

QUESTIONS FOR REFLECTION
- Where have I seen "vandal behavior" quietly tolerated at work? What message did that send to me or others?
- How does my team currently address active disengagement? Do we respond with avoidance, frustration, or intentional action?
- In what ways might I unknowingly be contributing to a culture of quiet resistance or negativity?
- What one step could I take this week to raise the standard, without gossiping or overstepping my role?
- If we eliminated just one "vandal influence" from our environment, how might that shift energy, trust, or momentum across the team?

CHAPTER 2
RENTERS BRING ONLY THEIR HANDS

In 2007, a great family moved into one of my properties. Let's call them the Williams. The dad was a state trooper. Mom was going back to school to get her dentistry degree. The two girls were in elementary school. They were ideal.

They moved from Tulsa to be close to the OU College of Dentistry school. The husband kept his same coverage area, so he drove over 90 minutes to work. He told me he loved being in his car and enjoyed the commute.

I rarely heard from them. They paid on time. They called me when they needed me. Otherwise, they kept to themselves. By then, their rent came through automated ACH transfers.

Four years after they moved in, the Williams moved out. The house looked the same, with a little wear and tear. Otherwise, it was almost as if they hadn't lived there. There were no improvements and minor deteriorations. I was grateful. Those with a renting mindset rarely enhance the space, but they maintain it. They preserve what's there even if they don't take initiative to improve it.

The Williams were there for a very specific purpose. It wasn't to settle down in a home. It was so mom could go to school. Then they could move somewhere she could build a practice and where they could establish their life. My home was just a means to an end. When they reached that end, they moved.

I've known plenty of people who approach work like the Williams. I once worked with Susan, a mid-level manager who was solid, dependable, productive, polite. But when a new opportunity came along, Susan left without any notice or knowledge transfer. No one got her files, her processes, or even a heads-up. She did a good job while she was there. But when she left, it was like she'd never really been part of the bigger picture. Just like the Williams family, Susan brought her skills, used the space, and moved on with no attachment.

RENTERS BRING ONLY THEIR HANDS

I've had many excellent tenants like the Williams. As the property manager, I met every person who applied. I gave the tours and ran all the background checks. In that process, two reasons jumped out as to why people rented:

1. Financial hardship due to medical bills.
2. Life transitions such as college graduation, marital status change, career change, or relocation.

From single moms to new couples to roommates, the people who lived in these houses were in transition. The homes didn't suffer damage, but they didn't get much love either. What they got was used. They were used for what that person or family needed and that was sufficient.

My tenants correctly saw the distinct advantages of renting:

1. Renting gives you opportunity to move from one place to the next with little consequence.
2. You aren't responsible for big broken items.
3. You don't have to make a large down payment with a long-term commitment.
4. You aren't responsible for the health of peripheral elements like the sewer line or the septic tank.
5. There is minimal future financial risk.

Like Susan, half of American workers are disengaged and operate with a renting mindset. They see their job simply as a means to an end, or a transitional stop on their way to a desired destination. Sometimes those renting in the workplace plan to move soon, or are uncertain about their future, so they hesitate to plant roots. Others see their whole career as a means to an end. They need money to live and meet their responsibilities. They work to get paid, and that's it. When they finally retire, their positions are like the house the Williams moved out of, undamaged, well used, and with no improvements made.

Just as renting has advantages in real estate, adopting a renter's mindset has advantages at work:

1. Renting gives you the opportunity to move from one job to another, with minimal attachment.
2. You aren't responsible for broken processes.
3. You don't invest your heart or head.
4. You don't own the responsibility for the health of the organization as a whole. Instead, you just do your job.
5. You don't tie yourself to future results.

Just like their housing counterparts, workplace renters enjoy the benefits of the not-my-problem attitude. However, they also miss out on the richer returns, because of their minimal investment.

One of the reasons people rent at work is because it gives them the freedom to jump to a new job with a higher pay. A lot of young people value the

BENEFITS OF RENTING

In Work	In Life
Opportunity for Job-Mobility	Consequence-Free Moves
Big Responsibilities Limited	Responsible for Small Items
Low Investment & Commitment	Low Investment & Commitment
Focus on You	No Extra Cares
Unattached to Future Results	Little Financial Risks

immediate gratification of that feeling. When they don't think they're being compensated fairly, they start looking for another opportunity elsewhere. You'll read more about that in Chapter 12. If someone is always looking for the next opportunity, they are not going to make major investments in their current position. They wouldn't have the time to do so, since applying for jobs takes tremendous effort.

It also relieves responsibility. Looking only at the position and duties, and not thinking about the organization as a whole, allows a person to say "I was only doing what I was told to do." They don't have to take any of the risks that come with making sacrificial investments. They don't stick their neck out to help fix a problem that isn't in their immediate scope of work.

To be clear, I'm not disparaging people with a renter's mindset at work. These individuals show up and typically do a good job, sometimes even a great one. They know what needs to be done. They know how to do it. They work consistently and reliably. They are literally half of the employees in the American workforce. They are driving the economic engine of society.

RENTERS DRIVE THE ECONOMIC ENGINE

Renters may enjoy their work. However, they've concluded it's not worth the extra effort to engage their hearts and minds. That is what they've "disengaged." Researchers define discretionary effort as the level of effort people could give, if they chose to (Zenger 2025). Gallup has found that engaged employees routinely participate 22% more than disengaged ones (Gallup Workplace n.d.). Renters rarely offer that extra effort. Not because they're unwilling, but because the culture has conditioned them not to. When initiative gets punished, discretionary effort gets buried.

In Part 2, we'll explore more thoroughly what return on investment at work looks like. Renters have realized either by experience or observation that what they "get back" for bringing an ownership mindset isn't a significant enough return to make it worth their while. Sometimes this may be a failure of their imagination. Sometimes, it's the organization's failure. If acting like an owner is not encouraged and rewarded, half of the workforce will make the rational choice not to bother with it.

WHY GIVE EVERYTHING WHEN THE REWARD IS THE SAME FOR GIVING HALF?

In fact, many people who attempt to innovate and try to make things better are dismissed. In organizations that perpetuate a renter's culture, those who bring an owner's mindset aren't appreciated.

When I say renters bring their hands only, I mean their skills, abilities, education, expertise, and experience. Renters bring all of these things to their work, but they don't bring their hearts and heads. They won't expand their investment beyond what is expected of them.

I worked with a small firm of about 150 employees. The leadership team consisted of five men who had been on staff an average of 20+ years. They all were competent and cared about the company as a whole, but petty rivalries created tension. One was jealous of another and didn't want to contribute to his team. It was incredibly unfortunate. These top leaders were all very knowledgeable and excellent at their individual tasks, but they didn't support each other. They didn't talk to each other. They didn't trust each other. It almost sounds like vandal behavior, but what you'll learn in Chapter 9 is that they each valued their room of the house more importantly than they valued the whole.

Not bringing heads and hearts isn't just about the organization itself. It also affects everyone on the team, no matter the role or position. A renter's mindset reduces people to their hands (the work they do) and ignores the deeper value of their head and heart.

I once worked with a guy who consistently complained in meetings that others weren't doing their job. What he really meant was that we weren't doing his job. He'd been there longer than most and had an attitude that he should get to do less work. It was bizarro to me. He didn't delegate, and the employees he tried to convince to do things weren't even in his department.

I cannot stress enough that those with a renter's mindset make up over 50% of the workforce and exist at every level of an organization. They aren't intentionally slowing anything down or holding progress back. If you have ever managed people at work, you know how valuable renters are. Having someone do a good job consistently is a great asset. But more is possible. Renting mindsets stabilize the organization, but they won't move it forward. Renters bring their hands, but the future belongs to those willing to bring their head and heart, too. To make progress, we need to shape cultures that offer a better value for investing heart, head, and hands, than simply keeping our job. Let's give those with a renter's mindset a good reason to start acting like owners.

QUESTIONS FOR REFLECTION
- In what ways have I seen "renter behavior" show up in my own work or on my team? What signals it most clearly?
- What might be motivating someone to rent instead of own at work? How could we reshape the environment to invite more ownership?
- What organizational habits or unspoken rules might unintentionally discourage people from giving their head and heart?
- Where am I doing a good job but not bringing extra thought or care? What would it look like to re-engage with purpose there?
- How might our team function if we started rewarding an ownership mindset more than just output?

CHAPTER 3
OWNERS BRING THEIR HEART, HEAD, AND HANDS

After the Williams family moved out, I had a flood of interest in the house. It really is a gem with three bedrooms and an office nestled at the back of a gated community. (It's not fancy, though. My daughter jokes, "Why does this neighborhood even need a gate?") It backs up to a greenbelt with a small creek winding through it. Trees. Quiet. Peaceful. Tucked away from traffic. I loved that house from the first time I walked through it.

The next family I moved in, the Donaldsons, would become one of the most meaningful stories of my real estate journey. The dad was a cop. The mom worked in HR while pursuing another degree. They had four kids ranging in age and full of energy. They rented that house for nine years.

What's wild is that even though they were renters, they lived in that house like they owned it. They painted rooms. Installed ceiling fans. Improved the landscaping. The dad would call me with things like, "*Hey Greg, I'm thinking about putting in a garden on the side of the house. That cool?*" I'd laugh and say, "Yes, please. Thank you!"

The Donaldsons didn't call with problems. They called with solutions. More often, they didn't call at all. I'd just show up and find a new improvement I didn't know about. I would try to reimburse them for materials, which they rarely took. Sometimes I didn't find out about fixes until years later.

One of the bigger issues with the house was drainage. Water pooled badly in the front corner of the yard, right beside the garage. A French drain had been installed, but it wasn't working. The dad got out there and dug the whole thing up himself. He mapped out the water flow, diagnosed the failure, and reengineered the solution. That's not just hard work, that's creativity and problem-solving in action. I told him I'd hire someone. He said, "That's gonna be expensive. I've got it."

Let me remind you, he was the tenant.

OWNERS BRING THEIR HEART, HEAD, AND HANDS

Inside the house, his wife showed the same care. The living room has three giant windows, each over two feet wide and ten feet tall. She made custom drapes—not out of necessity, but out of imagination. She wanted to create beauty, comfort, and character in the space. She wanted to craft a home.

They installed door hardware. Cared for animals from the greenbelt. Befriended the raccoons (turns out that keeps them out of the trash). Added beauty. Added function. Added life. They poured themselves into the place and I'm certain it gave something back.

The Donaldson's owner's mindset didn't end at the property line. They were *those* neighbors. The ones who knew everyone within six houses in every direction. They brought in the neighbors' garbage bins. Watched pets. Remembered birthdays. Built real community.

I've had great renters. I've had problematic renters. But the Donaldsons were owners in every sense of the word, even without a deed in hand.

⌂

Ownership is a mindset, not a legal status. We can bring it to anything, whether it's a house, a team, a business, a relationship, a mission.

I don't expect every renter to take initiative with my properties. But stories like the Donaldsons remind me that it's possible. I've seen hikers pick up other people's trash on trails they don't own. Neighbors plant flowers around shared entryways. Volunteers show up early and stay late to shape something they'll never "own" on paper.

OWNERSHIP IS A MINDSET

Acting like an owner isn't necessarily about possession. Sometimes, it's about care. And while care is the starting point, creativity is what transforms things from the ordinary. Owners don't just maintain, they imagine. They ask, *"What could this become?"*

For example, the City of Denver has an internal innovation team called Denver Peak Academy for frontline employees (City of Denver n.d.). Peak Academy trains people to think like owners, even when their role may seem more limited. The results are impressive. Over 3,500 improvements have been made directly from the team's ideas. A parking meter attendant redesigned how tickets were processed, saving thousands of dollars a month. A social worker restructured a service intake form that reduced wait times by hours. That's what happens when you support people to care for the organization.

OWNERS BRING THEIR HEART, HEAD, AND HANDS

One of the best-kept secrets of an ownership mindset is that it's more enjoyable. It just is. There's something deeply satisfying about investing in something, whether by improving it, beautifying it, or building it, even if it doesn't belong to you. In his book *Drive* (2011), Dan Pink calls this the power of autonomy, mastery, and purpose, the three pillars of lasting motivation. When we feel like we have ownership, we feel like we have *agency*. We make decisions. We solve problems. We care. And the result is fulfillment.

The old adage "leave it better than you found it" is more than a campsite motto. It's a way of living.

Do you know anyone who brings that kind of mindset to work? Someone who elevates their role, expanding the edges of their position instead of coloring just inside the lines? People like that bring their whole selves.

- They bring their heart: passion, energy, and care.
- Their head: imagination, critical thinking, and curiosity.
- And their hands: skill, ability, and expertise.

Those who act like owners bring all three! For the sake of the vision, clients, colleagues, and themselves, they invest their best. They care about the mission, the people, the process, and the results. And you can feel it.

At Barry-Wehmiller, a mid-sized manufacturing company based in St. Louis, leadership intentionally fosters a culture where employees feel safe and expected to act like owners (Chapman and Sisodia 2015). In one instance, a plant worker noticed a recurring equipment issue that slowed down production. Rather than waiting for management, he pulled in a few colleagues and redesigned a key part of the process, saving the company hundreds of hours annually. Then the company did something important. It recognized and celebrated the behavior. When people are trusted and expected to lead, they gravitate towards an ownership mindset.

We've briefly explored the three prevailing mindsets at work. Owners, renters, and vandals. As I said in the introduction, they aren't fixed. We can move from one to another, and we can inhabit different mindsets in different parts and seasons of our lives.

For instance, I'm a car vandal.

OWNERS BRING THEIR HEART, HEAD, AND HANDS

I own my vehicle, but I treat it like I'm trying to get it to rebel against me. I rarely clean it. I put off oil changes. I buy cheap fuel. One of the struts has been out for two years. The mechanic told me it wasn't essential, and I took that as a permanent green light.

So when it comes to cars, I bring an experienced vandal mindset. Ugh!

What about you? Where are you showing up as an owner? Where are you just going through the motions? Are you causing division, destruction, or strife anywhere?

The good news is that mindsets aren't permanent. They shift, evolve, and can be altered.

In Part 2, we'll dig into the Five Unlocks of the owner's mindset. Over the last decade I have tried and tested them in a variety of settings. They've created impact in mom and pop shops as well as Fortune 500 companies, and everywhere in between. What I've learned:

- People don't need to be convinced to care.
- They need a culture that rewards care and a space that welcomes imagination.
- They need a framework that invites both action and insight.
- They need leaders who embody it.

ACT LIKE AN OWNER

We want deeper meaning from our organizations. We want our work to be more satisfying. And we'd certainly like the liberties of the Donaldsons, being empowered to find creative solutions to problems, benefiting directly from our investments, and having full support from leadership. That's coming next.

Congrats, you just completed Part 1. Keep turning the pages to discover how the Unlocks apply to you and your organization.

QUESTIONS FOR REFLECTION
- Where am I bringing only my hands to work? What would it look like to bring my head and heart too?
- Who on my team consistently shows up like an owner? What behaviors make that obvious?
- How might our culture be unintentionally discouraging imagination, problem-solving, or initiative?
- What's one area in my role where I could stop waiting and start creating?
- If our whole team acted more like the Donaldsons, what kind of transformation could we see?

PART 2
THE FIVE UNLOCKS OF AN OWNER'S MINDSET

CHAPTER 4
IT GOES BOTH WAYS

We've laid the groundwork. We've explored the vandals who wreck culture, the renters who show up but don't buy in, and the owners who bring their full selves. In Part 1, we used the metaphor to describe what's happening in our organizations. But we don't want to just describe what's happening. We want to change what's happening. We want to increase engagement and fulfillment. In Part 2, we're going to explore the ownership values that will shape our future.

In my work with clients I've identified Five Unlocks that I consistently see in leaders, teams, and organizations who possess an ownership mindset:

ACT LIKE AN OWNER

1. **RISK BOLD COMMITMENTS**
2. **ACTIVATE LASTING VALUE**
3. **REACH FOR RESPONSIBILITY**
4. **WIDEN THE CIRCLE**
5. **THINK WHOLE HOUSE**

These aren't one-off behaviors or inspirational ideas you hear on a podcast and forget by lunch. These are the markers of a mindset. They create strong traction in real life. These traits apply to both people *and* organizations. Because both can choose to operate with an owner's mindset.

Here's where the metaphor gets tricky. A house is inanimate. It doesn't reciprocate. You can pour your heart, money, and time into it, but it's not going to invest in you back.

Yet we *talk* like it does. "This house has been so good to us." "It's taken care of our family."

Poetic? Sure. But it's not literally true. A house can shelter you, but it can't believe in you, support your dreams, or send you a thank-you card for fixing the sink.

Organizations, though? Different story.

Organizations are living organisms. They're built by people. Run by people. *For* people. They have values. Priorities. Choices. They can care ... or not. They can help you thrive...or suck the life out of you. That is the critical distinction. An organization can adopt an ownership mindset, too.

Some don't. Some do.

Some organizations rent their people. They treat them like tools, valuable only for what they produce. The minute the tool no longer works, they release them.

Others go full vandal. They chew people up, exploit their abilities, ignore their growth, steal their time, and then wonder why no one's loyal. They operate like it's the 19th-century coal industry. Sadly, they're still around.

THE BEST ORGANIZATIONS INVEST

They promote from within.
They care about health and well-being.
They educate their employees and develop their skills.
They build long-term relationships.
They prioritize people over policies.
They shape a space where contribution thrives.
They model what they want to see.
They act like an owner and it shows.

Simon Sinek (2014) puts this powerfully, "The leaders who get the most out of their people are the leaders who care most about their people." When an owner's mindset starts at the top, it cascades downward.

A great example of this caring comes from one of my clients, Smith + Howard in Atlanta. When COVID struck, many companies scrambled to figure out how to make remote work happen. Smith + Howard had core values that honored their people and provided resources for them to succeed. Immediately, they took what everyone's workstation included and replicated it in their home office with ergonomic chairs, computers, cameras, etc. It was a HUGE investment that paid off in spades. Employees and partners greatly appreciated the quick, generous decision from leadership and worked their hardest to make remote work effective. The company cared and when it mattered most, they showed up and acted according to their values.

This demonstrates how an ownership culture goes both ways. There is reciprocity when people feel seen by their organization's leadership. It also reveals how workplace culture operates beyond the walls. Value-based-decisions aren't confined to a specific building or location. (More on this in chapter 13.)

Another company that has demonstrated the power of reciprocity is Menlo Innovations, a tech company based in Michigan led by CEO Richard Sheridan. The leadership team made an unusual but powerful decision when they committed to joy in the workplace as a non-negotiable value (Sheridan 2013). Joy was embedded in their daily operations and treated as essential to performance. This commitment shaped how they structured teams, managed projects, and led people.

Even when facing tight deadlines or high-stakes client demands, Menlo refused to compromise the practices that protected their culture. They held firmly to pair programming, clean handoffs, and what they affectionately called team sanity. For them, success was measured by both deliverables and how they got there. Their conviction is clear that a joyful, respectful, human-centered process leads to better outcomes and a stronger team.

In Part 3, we'll talk more about how to create an ownership culture throughout an organization. Here's a sneak peek. When organizations lead with an ownership mindset, employees are far more likely to show up with one, too. Commitment begets commitment. Ownership flows both ways. It's not a gimmick or a feel-good strategy, it's reciprocity at work.

IT HAS TO GO BOTH WAYS

WHAT IT TAKES TO GROW

There's a decent chance you've felt taken advantage of at work. Maybe not, but odds are, you have. A leader's job is to get the best out of you, and that requires stretching. This happens outside of your comfort zone.

That doesn't mean exploiting you. It means expanding you.

A great coach doesn't let you cruise. They challenge you to level up. Same with a great leader. They'll stretch you. If you're not careful, you might misinterpret that stretch as mistreatment. But often, it's the push you didn't know you needed. Your resistance might cause you to miss the chance to enlarge your capacity in ways that could open new doors for you.

That kind of growth is costly. It's hard becoming someone you're currently not.

People love to talk about the "best version of themselves," like it's magically waiting for them in a future season. That version of you is built, not discovered. Growth demands sacrifice. "Best versions" require more than "normal versions."

If you think your company is unfairly extracting your time, energy, or creativity, pause. You might be missing an incredible development opportunity. The people who get this realize that no one can take advantage of

IT'S HARD BECOMING WHAT YOU'RE NOT YET

you when you own your role. You're not being used. You're *choosing* to show up, to grow, and to bring value, both to your organization and yourself.

This mindset opens a kind of freedom most people never experience. When you bring your full self (heart, head, hands) you take charge of your future. Not because work is easy, but because you're worth it and hopefully the work is too.

The next chapters explore each Unlock of an ownership mindset. As we step into them, I invite you to bring your audacity. I'm not writing this so a leader somewhere can weaponize these traits and squeeze more productivity out of you. I'm writing this so *you* can build your best, most meaningful life. A life where you're not a victim. Not stuck. Not powerless. A person who walks into any room, any challenge, any failure, any hard conversation, and owns your role with persistence, clarity, and joy.

This isn't about pleasing your boss. This is about choosing to live with intention in every meeting, every conversation, every missed deadline, every team conflict. You're not powerless. You have agency!

These upcoming chapters will act as a compass to point you in the direction that leads you towards a fulfilling future.

ACT LIKE AN OWNER

When a company gets this and shapes a culture where ownership thrives, it becomes magnetic. Performance goes up and to the right. People stay, grow, and buy-in. Culture becomes a competitive advantage.

QUESTIONS FOR REFLECTION
- How does my organization currently show care or investment in its people? Where might it still be renting or vandalizing?
- What's one recent decision I've seen that reflected an ownership mindset from leadership? What impact did it make?
- In what ways am I showing up with ownership, even when the organization doesn't always seem reciprocal?
- How could we, as a team, create more spaces where people feel safe to contribute, imagine, and improve things?
- When have I confused being stretched with being mistreated? What growth might be hiding in that discomfort?

CHAPTER 5
RISK BOLD COMMITMENTS

In 2001 in Edmond, Oklahoma, I was sitting inside a small room with a conference table that had lots of pens. I had been ushered back here by a kind lady who'd offered me all kinds of snacks and sodas. I was nervous. I'd never purchased a home I wasn't going to live in and now I was getting ready to sign a 30-year mortgage and invest over $15,000 cash.

My closing agent Shawna exhibited enormous patience as I read through every document I was required to sign or initial. There were a lot. It felt like I was taking the biggest risk of my life purchasing a $77,000 house.

As a 3 bed, 2 bath, 1350 square feet corner lot home, I imagine you are gasping at how low the price was. Remember it was 2001 and Edmond is one of the least expensive places to live in America. Everything is relative. Fifteen thousand dollars was a lot of money to me. It felt like a big risk!

Then Mike moved in. (Remember him? He's the guy who disappeared.) Mike paid a $600 deposit and signed a one-year lease. Significantly less than my investment. He didn't need to take the risk because he was only going to remain temporarily (little did I know *how* temporarily). That's one of the advantages of being a renter, minimal future financial risk.

In contrast, being an owner requires being willing to risk. I sank a large chunk of cash into the house, took on a 30-year mortgage, and I put my credit on the line.

This is the first Unlock of an ownership mindset.

RISK BOLD COMMITMENTS

How does this apply to the workplace? Unless you're an entrepreneur, hopefully you aren't risking your credit or sinking cash into your job (though there are a lot of teachers who buy their own school supplies). What, then, does the risk of commitment look like?

Let's start with what commitment *doesn't* mean.

Every employer would love to have commitment from their

employees. However, most don't articulate well what that looks like or the benefits of being deeply committed. Unfortunately, most use time as their primary indicator of someone's commitment level. And that's a really bad idea.

TIME IS A POOR ASSESSMENT!

Just because someone has worked at an organization for decades doesn't mean they're committed. They may just be someone with a high tolerance for pain who has figured out how to work the system. Or they could be a mentor who passes on institutional knowledge to new employees. It could go either way. That's why time in itself is an inaccurate way to measure commitment.

Time "in the office" during the week is used as a measure of commitment as well. Someone will say "I'm the first one in and the last one out. I work weekends. I'm obviously committed!" My response is, "Well ... maybe. Or you might just be slow at your job. What takes you twelve hours to do, others get done in six." Just because you work long hours doesn't mean you're committed to the mission of the organization, the success of your clients or the growth of your colleagues. On the other hand, you might wake up every day excited to live out your purpose at work and you just can't stay away! It could go either way. Again, time is not an effective way to measure legitimate commitment.

Melissa was a regional manager for a chain of retail stores. On paper, she was a rockstar. She worked 70+ hours a week, visited multiple store locations each month, jumped in to cover callouts, and fielded emails from employees at all hours of the night. If the company handed out trophies for "most visibly committed," Melissa would have had a shelf full of them.

Her regional VP started noticing that despite all the hustle, her team had the highest turnover in the company. Exit interviews told the same story over and over. "She never trusts us." "She does everything herself." "She doesn't want input; she only wants obedience." "She's burning out, and burning us out with her."

Melissa wasn't committed to the mission of the company. She was committed to control. She didn't empower her team, she micromanaged them. She didn't build capacity, she took over. It's not that she didn't care … she did. She cared a lot. But mostly about keeping things "done her way."

If someone made a mistake, Melissa wouldn't coach or develop them, she'd take the task away. Over time, the team stopped trying. They did the bare minimum, kept their heads down, and quietly looked for other jobs.

RISK BOLD COMMITMENTS

From a distance, Melissa looked like the ultimate owner. But in reality, she was renting with a martyr complex, doing all the work herself and quietly resenting everyone for not matching her pace.

Know anyone like that?

What are the metrics of commitment at your work? What behaviors do you model and look for in others that reveal a deep commitment to where you're going as an organization and to the development of the people getting you there? I imagine when you drill down on what they are, you'll come up with some very specific attributes.

In my work I have found two tangible, measurable traits that are consistent in the lives of individuals who are leading and living with commitment, *contribution* and *accountability*.

CONTRIBUTION

Almost everyone starts out day one on their job with an owner's mindset. They show up ready and wanting to prove their worth. Determined to let their leaders, managers, colleagues, and direct reports know that they are competent and capable of the task at hand, they contribute thoughts and ideas vigorously.

We've all been in meetings when the new guy shows up.

Let's call him New Guy because he appears in every workplace. He comes in ablaze with energy and excitement, jazzed to be there. He's done his homework and he's ready to participate and make things better. He starts sharing ideas, asking questions, referencing TEDtalks, mentioning podcasts, all with the hope of proving he is going to be a valuable teammate!

Of course, everyone else in the meeting is thinking, or even saying in so many words, "Simmer down skippy, we're going to crush your soul and squash your dreams very soon." They just want to get through the meeting and get back to work, while New Guy thinks he can make a difference.

That happens for a short period of time, until New Guy learns to just keep quiet and not share his ideas. He pulls back and focuses solely on his work and not the big picture. In his mind he thinks "Fine, I won't share my ideas or experiences any more with you. I've been interfacing with clients and know I could help solve a problem, but I'll just keep it to myself."

Persistently contributing feels risky. It can alienate those who have stopped trying. Contribution is an expression of care. If we stop contributing, we stop caring, which leads us to stop being committed.

WITHOUT CONTRIBUTION YOU WON'T SUSTAIN COMMITMENT!

RISK BOLD COMMITMENTS

This is the perversity of organizations. They want people to buy in, yet the very thing that creates a sense of ownership, they snuff out. They violate reciprocity. New Guy is trying his best to give something meaningful for the success of the organization. Leadership does not always do its best to receive, cherish, and utilize that energy.

On top of that, supervisors turn around and blame the individual. During New Guy's first annual review, they'll say something like "you started out so strong, then you seemed to withdraw and stop caring. What happened?" He thinks to himself, "I started working here!"

Some new employees play a role in undermining their own contributions. They start out with lots of ideas, then take it personally when those suggestions are not immediately implemented. The organization shouldn't squash a new employee's energy, but being open to their ideas doesn't require acting on them immediately or even at all.

Most of us are really attached to our ideas. We get excited about sharing them. We're convinced we have a smart, magical solution. It's hard when we enthusiastically share them and they land flat... or worse, gets shot down with equal enthusiasm.

Immature people connect their identity to their ideas. Mature professionals know that concepts are cheap. They come and go, with new ones appearing daily. The hard work is deciding on the right one, developing it, and then executing with excellence.

Unfortunately, sometimes we get our feelings hurt or get offended when our notion is not received with the same hope and excitement with which we offered it. Let me save us all some heartache and share a hard truth.

We have mostly bad ideas. Let me say it again … most of our ideas are bad. I can promise you this, we have no great ideas on our own and it's unlikely we even have a good idea. At best, we have a mediocre opinion. (Feel free to make copies of this page so you can hand it to someone in your meeting and say, "*I'm* not saying this, but Greg has a thought about what you just offered.")

YOU HAVE BAD IDEAS

I know, I know … you think I'm wrong and you have proof about some amazing idea you or your co-worker had in the past. Or you think you regularly bring smart insights. Nope. Well, maybe on a rare occasion. Mostly, we all have bad ideas. They only become good ideas when others start beating them up, stretching them apart, and adding their perspective. We only form a great idea when multiple people from multiple areas have contributed to it. We won't know till we field test it, and from there, make adjustments that enable it to be a fabulous solution.

BRILLIANT SOLUTIONS ARE JUST BAD IDEAS MADE BETTER TOGETHER!

Not consensus, but contribution. Conversations that question, disagree and challenge. Amazing solutions lie hidden in conflict or uncomfortable discourse. See why it feels risky?

.: NOTE to LEADERS :.
For those of you who lead meetings or brainstorming sessions, I suggest you start by saying, "I have a few bad ideas to suggest …" It takes your ego out of the equation and encourages everyone else to be willing to share their ideas, even if they don't think they're that good. This stops people from self-censoring. Many won't share seeds of a potentially powerful thought because they're afraid of how they'll be perceived and treated.
.: END NOTE :.

We want people to contribute, contribute, contribute. It solidifies commitment and keeps heads and hearts engaged. The challenge is nurturing a culture that says "We want to hear all of your ideas," while simultaneously acknowledging that 80–90% of the time the immediate response is NO. Whether it's because of budget, manpower, or timelines, all valid reasons, it can feel like rejection to the contributor.

It's important for the leader to find ways to communicate "not now" with the hope and intention of finding opportunities to quickly implement someone's solution that has the potential to create big results.

.: NOTE to LEADERS :.

It's important to demonstrate you sharing an idea, vision or solution that gets put on the shelf for another time, too. Create a culture where everyone knows the answer is normally "Love that! Thank you. Probably not right now, but let's explore possibilities in the future." Of course, if it's an immediate solution for an urgent need, utilize it now. Also, you actually do have to go back and revisit the Vault of Ideas, demonstrating that you treasure people's contributions. Make the vault public, so others can peruse it as well, hopefully finding ways to build on an original thought.

.: END NOTE :.

At all costs, keep an environment that encourages, supports, and requires contribution from everyone! If an organization never accepts input from its employees, they will stop contributing and adopt an attitude of learned helplessness. They realize that their thoughts don't matter and someone else will make all the decisions (Seligman 1975).

RISK BOLD COMMITMENTS

BAD IDEA TO VALUABLE SOLUTION
How Collaborative Refinement Improves Your Idea.

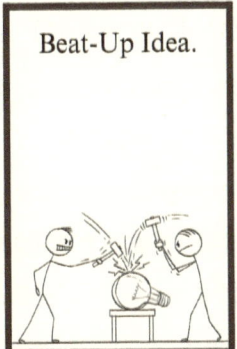

Disengagement starts the day a person holds back an idea. When people stop contributing, they withdraw commitment ... and so begins their journey into renting. The issue with Melissa's work is not that she didn't put in the hours. It's that she did so much that she didn't leave any room for her employees' own contributions, and they became disengaged. She practically forced them to be renters.

Conversely, if an organization welcomes contributions from all of its employees, it sets itself up for more ideas than it knows what to do with. A few of them might even produce significant advances! Remember Menlo Park and Denver Peak Academy?

At W. L. Gore & Associates, Gore-Tex, one of the company's most iconic innovations—the waterproof, breathable fabric—was introduced by an employee who saw a need and stepped forward with a solution. Gore & Associates' lattice structure is hailed by Gary Hamel in *The Future of Management* (2007) for its capacity to spark innovation. Employees are trusted to speak up, take initiative, and move ideas forward without needing prior approval. That practice reflects a culture of ownership in its purest form.

When people understand that ideas have to go through a rigorous proving ground before they can be implemented, that most thoughts are not ready yet, and that instead of "no" we say "not now," then they are encouraged to inhabit an owner's mindset.

Contributions are an essential part of ownership. Imagine that you owned a house, but because of strict historical preservation laws, you were not allowed to change a single thing about it. Imagine further that you weren't even allowed to clean it or move around any furniture because of its historic value. Only outside professionals would be allowed to do anything to it and you couldn't make any decisions about it.

This wouldn't be owning a home. It would be living in a museum. The ability to contribute to the upkeep, maintenance, and improvement of your home is an essential part of the ownership mindset, as the Donaldson family demonstrated.

So too, in the workplace, the ability to contribute to the mission of the organization is essential to having an owner's mindset.

△

ACCOUNTABILITY

The other powerful indicator of risking bold commitments is *accountability*. We hear this word a lot, but often don't find an effective way for it to be realized in workplaces. There are two reasons for this.

First, the very essence of accountability means we must acknowledge that we need HELP in an area of our life. Our egos resist that wholeheartedly. We're professionals. Some of us have been doing this a long time. Asking for help seems both like admitting weakness and confessing that we've been bringing less-than-our-best in our current role.

Unfortunately, organizations try to require accountability programs for their employees, sometimes in punitive rather than empowering ways. How would you and I react if forced to participate in a potentially threatening accountability program aimed right at our vulnerabilities?

Not well, not willing, and certainly not wanting. We'd make sure we looked good and only reveal very small flaws that are easy to fix. In other words, we're not going to do accountability for real. We won't expose our persistent weaknesses, haunting deficiencies, or glaring gaps which is the very thing we must do to make meaningful progress.

This is why accountability programs only work when they're freely chosen. It's such a risk. When accountability is invited by both parties,* it enables us to become what we can't on our own. It is extremely difficult to become something we're not.

---

* To be clear, this is not the same thing as a PIP or HR initiated response to certain unwelcome behaviors.

Knowledge doesn't change us. Observing others won't get us there. Learning tips, tricks, and strategies won't do it. Determined, disciplined

WE NEED HELP TO IMPROVE

actions are what cause us to become what we're currently not. Not vision. Not aspiration. Not hope. Not desire. Only determined, disciplined actions. And without someone beside us, it's unlikely we'll maintain the rigorous routines required.

Human nature rests at mediocrity. Left on our own for any length of time, we drift towards average. We can only sustain excellence with accountability, a nudge from someone else to remind us of who we want to be.

WITHOUT ACCOUNTABILITY YOU WON'T SUSTAIN EXCELLENCE!

Most of us think of an "accountability partner" as someone we go and confess our sins to regarding where we failed or didn't measure up. That perspective is one of the reasons people resist being held accountable. Who wants to be reminded weekly of where we fail?

We also tend to think one person holds us accountable in every area. However, since we all have unique strengths and weaknesses, it makes more sense to look to individuals to help us improve different aspects of our skillset and thinking.

I prefer to use the term "Progress Partner." When we want to make progress in a particular area, we invite a person into our life who excels in that area and ask them to partner with us so we can become who we want to be. Accountability is the primary tool for making progress.

PROGRESS PARTNER
POSSIBLE AREAS OF PROGRESS

- IMPROVING COMMUNICATION
- BETTER DECISION MAKING
- DELEGATING EFFECTIVELY
- LEARNING NEW SKILLS
- CREATING CONSISTENCY
- EXPANDING PERSPECTIVE
- GROWING NETWORK
- EMPOWERING WELL
- ENERGY LEVELS
- TAKING RISKS

The second reason it's hard to make accountability work at work is because it is uncomfortable to hold someone accountable. Progress partners have to be willing to enforce real consequences if an agreed-upon goal is not reached. If your colleague says "I want you to hold me to the standard of making all my meetings on time, no matter what. If I don't, I'll pay you five dollars for every minute I'm late," you might feel a bit guilty taking their money the next time they're ten minutes late for a meeting. They'll have a reason or excuse, but that's not the point. Holding someone accountable is about whether the desired behaviors are demonstrated.

Accountability is an agreement between two people, and consequences are part of that agreement. It gets awkward imposing those consequences. Since we all have our own areas of suckage, we tend to be a bit merciful towards colleagues who are trying, who mean well and want to do better, but their actions aren't there yet. Of course, progress partners shouldn't get excited about causing pain either. The right progress partner will strike a firmly gracious balance.

That's exactly why accountability is an indicator of risking bold commitments. As individuals we are vying and vowing to press for continual improvement. Why would we invite this painful process at work unless we were committed to growth, determined to excel as professionals, and eager to serve our clients well?

INVITE ACCOUNTABILITY

An extreme example of peer-led accountability comes from The Morning Star Company, a tomato processing company in California. Morning Star operates without bosses. Instead of traditional hierarchy, every employee writes a personal mission statement and makes peer-to-peer commitments that guide their work. Accountability is negotiated directly with colleagues through self-created contracts. No one assigns tasks or dictates directions. This model works because accountability is both personal and public. Everyone knows what others have committed to, and everyone is expected to follow through (Morgan 2014; Hamel 2011).

Granted, that's an outlier approach. However, it demonstrates what's possible when individuals risk bold commitments and organizations create an ownership culture that models agency, transparency, and trust.

Let's establish what it looks like to be committed in your team, department, or organization. Clearly defining the metrics of commitment, enables organizations to shape a culture that empowers individuals to act like owners.

When time is removed as the primary measurement and more accurate standards like contribution and accountability are

articulated, individuals will risk bold commitments!

Like my $15,000 down payment it may not seem like much to you. But to the person

RISK BOLD COMMITMENTS

making the commitment, it feels very risky!

Understandably then, organizations must be equal partners with the employee, by:

- Reciprocating and truly welcoming contributions.
- Providing a non-punitive structure for accountability focused on progress, growth, and expanding capabilities.

When this kind of partnership flourishes, purpose and productivity thrive!

QUESTIONS FOR REFLECTION
- What does commitment look like in our organization beyond time or tenure? How clearly is that defined or modeled?
- When have I stepped back from contributing because my idea was dismissed or ignored? What mindset shift would help me re-engage?
- Where could I invite someone to be a "progress partner" to help me grow in a specific area at work?
- What are we doing as a team to reward risk-taking, idea-sharing, and healthy accountability?
- If contribution and accountability are the true metrics of commitment, how do I measure up in both? What needs to change?

CHAPTER 6
ACTIVATE LASTING VALUE

I loved the second home I ever bought. It was a two-story with a quirky layout, built in 1983, just over 1900 square feet, and packed with character. Like many newbies, I rented it to four college guys who destroyed it. My infamous #VandalHouse. ☹

After a few rough renters, I eventually leased it to what I affectionately called the Brady Bunch family. The mom brought a few kids, the dad brought a few more—seven or eight total, all under one roof. The house was bursting with zany energy.

The mom stayed home and ran the whole operation. She managed the schedules, cooked the meals, did the laundry, and tracked chores on a poster board in the living room with stars and color-coded tasks.

Their dining table was a picnic table. Not a fancy one from Pottery Barn or West Elm. It looked like it was yanked from a city park. It appeared to be industrially built to endure weather and wild children. It fit the family perfectly.

One day, the dad called me. "Greg, the oven's arcing."

Now, for context, let me explain my real estate strategy. It is a simple two-step approach.

1. Buy Nice Houses
2. Put Nice People in Them

That's it. I have zero handyman skills. Every time I try to fix something, I make it worse and cost myself more money. So I hire everything out. My strategy to invest in quality homes and quality people has worked for a couple of decades.

Back to the oven. I went over to see what was going on. While I couldn't fix it, I still wanted to understand the problem. The dad turned it on, and sure enough, a spark would leap across the bottom burner. It had corroded and dissolved. After 30 years of faithful service, it was done.

I told him to turn it off, and that I'd buy them a replacement.

ACTIVATE LASTING VALUE

While we were talking, the mom walked in and casually added, "Ummm ... Greg, only one of the four burners on the stove works."

Wait, what?!

This woman cooked two full meals a day, every day, for a family of eight, on one burner. I stood there stunned, picturing her running back and forth between the stove and that massive picnic table. Pork chops, green beans, another side ... all cooked one pan or pot at a time.

At first, I was baffled. Why hadn't she told me?

People want to make their life and work better. You do. I do. We all want to increase the value of the things around us.

I realized her unwillingness to share with me was a combination of two things. First, she was afraid to tell me. She probably didn't trust how I would respond. She may have imagined that telling me about the broken burners would lead to blame,

PEOPLE AVOID THE TRUTH BECAUSE IT'S NOT SAFE

judgment, or a financial penalty. Once she saw how I reacted to the oven—calm, helpful, no drama—she felt safe enough to bring up the burners. People don't avoid telling the truth because they don't care. They avoid it because they don't feel safe.

I thought I was a great landlord. Turns out, she didn't fully trust my response, so she chose to endure inconvenience and settle for mediocrity. I may have prevented her from bringing an ownership mindset because she didn't feel safe enough to contribute. Or it could have simply been a story she told herself about landlords that had nothing to do with me personally.

This happens in organizations regularly. Many leaders get frustrated with employees and assume they know why people are hiding problems, making poor decisions, or underperforming. The truth is, people aren't careless. *They're cautious.* They would rather take their chances with the fallout of a bad decision than risk the emotional pain of embarrassment, disappointment, retaliation or punishment of being publicly called out.

We've seen this play out in deeply sobering ways, even in industries where safety should never be compromised. Boeing once had a culture grounded in engineering integrity. Safety was sacred. Employees were encouraged to speak up and they did. But after its 1997 merger with McDonnell Douglas, something shifted (Robison 2021). Pressure to cut costs began to outweigh the commitment to caution. Deadlines started driving decisions. Engineers who once had a voice were now overruled or ignored. Concerns were minimized, and essential software changes were approved without shared clarity or full consensus.

Then came the unthinkable. Two 737 Max crashes claimed

hundreds of lives. Investigators ultimately discovered the cause went beyond flawed software or failed systems. It was cultural. Fear had replaced ownership. Silence had replaced courage.

It's a painful but powerful reminder that when people no longer feel safe to speak up, everyone is at risk. Cultures that elevate speed over safety, or compliance over contribution, may seem efficient, but the hidden cost is trust. And without trust, value shrinks, truth hides, and tragedy has room to take root.

What is essential for all cultures is what Harvard researcher Amy Edmondson calls psychological safety (2018), a shared belief that the team is safe for interpersonal risk-taking. Her research shows it's the single most important predictor of high-performing teams. When safety disappears, so does honesty and truth. And it's hard for an organization to make the best decisions to further its mission when it doesn't know the truth.

If we want people to activate lasting value, we must first make it safe for them to do so.

What was the other reason the Brady Bunch mom didn't tell me about the stove? Even if someone feels safe, they may still feel *powerless*. She had settled into a belief that nothing could be done. That things couldn't change. That a broken-down stove was just the way it was going to be. She didn't have the resources to fix it herself, and she didn't feel like she had the authority to ask for help. So she adapted and accepted mediocrity as the standard. She thought to herself "this is just how it has to be."

It's the same belief that plagues employees who say, "What am I supposed to do about it? I don't get a say in the budget. I don't have the authority to tell people what to do!"

Most of us bump into things at work that frustrate us, like inefficiencies, broken systems, and unhealthy dynamics. They feel beyond our reach to resolve. How can we make it better? We don't have the budget. We don't have the title. So we shrug and settle for a strategy of mediocrity.

Consider this mindshift.

Even without authority or budget, you can activate lasting value consistently in your work place.

How, you ask?

 FREE WORDS

From the frontline to the C-suite, every person can increase their value and the value of others through words that cost nothing but mean everything.

It is called setting the **BAR**, where small acknowledgments spark trust and elevate culture:

BEHAVIORS
Notice and affirm someone, doing something right.

ATTITUDE
Recognize a positive mindset in a tough moment.

RESPONSES
Highlight disciplined, calm or wise choices under pressure.

Here's a shining example that illustrates the power of Responses. According to a Harvard Business Review article on *reflective recognition* (Littlefield 2021), leaders at one fast-growing restaurant chain often began weekly leadership meetings by asking each manager, "What are you proud of from last week?" These meetings consistently revealed high-impact actions that might otherwise have gone unnoticed. Like a training manager who spent late nights fine-tuning a new program while managing customer demands. When asked to reflect, she realized the creativity and endurance required to launch it successfully. Her leader then publicly praised the effort to highlight how her problem-solving mindset protected both staff and guests. That Response moment became a defining cultural pulse. People began paying attention to good, sometimes small, contributions and naming them out loud.

We can activate lasting value simply by paying attention, then communicating our observations. I challenge my consulting clients to pick one person a week to observe. Make mental or written notes. Then, intentionally say something specific and encouraging. Three powerful things happen when you do.

1. THE PERSON FEELS SEEN

Being seen is one of the strongest emotional needs we all carry. Validation communicates that someone is mindful, understands, and empathizes with your experience, essentially saying, *"I get you. You matter."* Emotional validation defuses negative feelings, builds trust, and shows someone that their effort did not go unnoticed.

Acknowledgment of positive behaviors and good choices is incredibly affirming (Fleck 2025). Research shows that visible support during moments of stress leads to immediate improvements in well-being. But it goes deeper than simply feeling better. When someone says, "I saw that," it releases bonding hormones like oxytocin, making the recipient feel safe and connected.

That simple act of recognition with words like "I noticed

how you courageously led that conversation," or "I appreciate the positivity you brought today" ignites the soul of the receiver. It says, your contribution matters and I see you at your best. That feeling is transformative! It elevates people, teams, and the culture of an organization.

Founder and CEO Cheri Garcia of Cornbread Hustle embodies this. Cornbread Hustle is an employment agency for second chances. Cheri has created a culture that sees beyond what someone did in the past and recognizes their intrinsic value in the present and future. Concerning her approach to seeing each person as they are, Cheri shared with me.

> *We open up our interviews by being vulnerable and sharing something about our past. (All of us are either formerly incarcerated or in recovery) This has been the most simple way to make someone feel seen without them even having to tell us anything. We become vulnerable to minimize the shame and/or fear someone feels during an interview. More often than not, someone is relieved that they can be themselves and openly share about their criminal record in an interview without as much fear.*

One of the brilliant things about Cheri's approach is that she has found a way to use free words to recognize someone else by sharing her own vulnerability. This can be an effective approach to validate someone, both in more serious contexts such as Cheri's case, and in everyday cases as well. "Maria, can you show me how you organize your email? I really struggle with that and you are always so on top of everything."

2. THE PERSON RECIPROCATES LIKING

Read this slowly.

People Like People Who Like Them.

Now, say it out loud (even more slowly).

That might be the most important sentence in this chapter. Maybe in the whole book.

You don't need to be wildly charismatic. You don't need to be everyone's best friend. You don't have to participate in every gathering. You just need to like people.

I always have an advantage when I'm speaking. Everyone in the audience is determining whether they like me. They'll look, listen, and experience me for a bit before they make a determination. I start out liking everyone in the audience. The mistake most leaders (and people) make is they decide if they like someone based on who or how that person is ... and most of the time they'll see things that are different. And differences create distance

PEOPLE LIKE PEOPLE WHO LIKE THEM

The strategy I use, which is now engrained in me, is to like others based on who I am,* not on who they are. When I do that, I consistently find things about them that are similar or likable. I'm telling you, it is magical. *(I'm the kind of person who chooses to like you completely, simply because you are you.)

I know, I know ... you might be thinking, "I don't really like them and I don't care if they like me." Quick fact, people don't trust people they don't like. So it's not like I want people to like me so we can hang out after work. I want to build likable relationships so when a difficult situation arises, there is enough trust between us that we deal directly with one another and resolve it as quickly and effectively as possible.

Using free words enables that to happen. It activates lasting value in you and them. This is backed by research published in *Harvard Business Review* which found that employees who

ACT LIKE AN OWNER

PEOPLE DON'T TRUST PEOPLE THEY DON'T LIKE understand how their work positively impacts others are significantly more motivated, engaged, and committed (Amabile and Kramer 2011). Just knowing that their contribution creates value for someone else drives performance and satisfaction.

.: NOTE to LEADERS :.

As a leader you don't get the option to not like the people you lead. (Should I say that again too?) If you're in leadership, the only disposition that is honorable and smart for business, is that you genuinely like everyone on your team. If in your mind you are arguing with me "but Greg, you don't know these yahoos I work with ..." you're right, I don't. But if you'll go back and re-read, liking the people you lead is all about YOU owning your role. Don't blame others for being different than you. Your unwillingness to be relationally smart is the problem, not them.

If you're going to persist in not liking those you lead, you are contributing to their disengagement and less than stellar contributions and results. If you doubt me, try it. Choose to sincerely like everyone you lead for three months. See if something doesn't change in their productivity.

.: END NOTE :.

If you want to active lasting value I dare you to say these

words to someone. "I like you." Not in a creepy or weird way. Genuinely and casually, utter that phrase. It strikes a nerve in every human. It has a reciprocating effect that's incredibly cool. There's research on it, but you can do your own experiments. It affects the heart and mind, the aspects of an owner's mindset we are trying to engage.

One caveat. It has to be true. That's why if you take on my philosophy of liking people based on who you are, instead of who they are, it can be authentic every time you say it. You'll actually mean it.

Warning. People aren't used to it, so they'll think you want something from them. You don't. (And if you do, none of the mystical magical responses will occur).

Let me say this one more time.

People Like People Who Like Them.

3. YOUR WORDS SHAPE THEIR IDENTITY.

Specific praise will change how a person sees themselves. I'm an encourager. I can walk in an office and spout off things like "You're awesome!," "You're doing a great job!," "Man, I really appreciate you!," "Love what you're doing!" These are NOT the kind of free words that will make a difference. That kind of "encouragement" is like a sugar hit. It can feel good in the moment, but can actually turn negative. You might have an "encourager" in your office and find them incredibly annoying or insincere.

Unfortunately, the human soul is wired in such a way that the negative sticks and the positive slips. Someone could have said something ugly to us ten, twenty, or even thirty years ago and it still remains in us. We can still hear it. Still feel it. For some, it's shaped our identity. For others it's limited our willingness to attempt certain things in life. Are you carrying negative words around with you? If so, you are unfortunately in the majority.

What stinks is that someone could have said something incredibly positive to you six months ago and it's already exited your memory. That doesn't seem right, does it? I'm sorry. I wish it weren't so, but it is. The good news is, there's a way to make the positive stick. Specificity is the secret to creating a long-term impact with your free words.

When you say "Hey Erin, I saw the way you responded to that customer yesterday. You were patient and firm and kept your cool. That was impressive, because they were acting ridiculous!"

"Hey Derrick, I noticed how you initiated three different ideas in the meeting today. That took courage and thoughtfulness. I love the way you addressed the challenges that

ACTIVATE LASTING VALUE

you knew would come up. It was really smart. I'm proud to be on the same team with you."

Specificity doesn't just inspire, it puts hooks in the soul. It anchors and remains. Whether we are a leader, colleague or subordinate, this is the greatest gift we can give someone. Pointing out and articulating stellar qualities that you see in them is a potentially life-altering experience.

SPECIFICITY PUTS HOOKS IN THE SOUL

Have you ever had someone see something in you that you didn't see in yourself? Have you ever had someone believe in you more than you believed in yourself? I hope so. It alters our perception. It infuses courage, hope, and belief. It activates lasting value.

That's where true motivation lies. Not "oh Greg said nice things about me, I'm going to do that more, so he says more nice things about me." That's not how motivation works. It's an internal stimulus. What really happens is the next time Erin has a difficult customer, it will be easier for her to respond with grace. Derrick will say, "Wow, I love the way Greg sees me. I want to be THAT kind of person all the time." And then he leans into that identity *for himself*, not for me, you, or anyone else.

When we paint a positive picture of how we see someone and share it with them, they want to continue to be that person.

Make a list of people you'd like to inspire over the coming months. Use the BAR to determine what to look for. Try this for ninety days and see what happens! You will activate lasting value in others and through the process you will become more valuable. When we set the BAR for others, we not only elevate their contribution, we elevate the culture we share. Choose to become someone who unlocks lasting impact in every room you enter. See the good, say the good, spark more of the good.

QUESTIONS FOR REFLECTION

- Where do I have the chance to activate lasting value with someone this week? What is keeping me from doing it?
- What would shift in our culture if every team member committed to "setting the BAR" with free words of encouragement?
- Do I believe my words can shape someone else's identity for the better? When has someone's shaped mine?
- When have I held back useful feedback or affirmation because I didn't feel like it mattered? What mindset shift do I need to make?
- How could we create rhythms or rituals as a team that make activating lasting value a regular practice?

CHAPTER 7
REACH FOR RESPONSIBILITY

When you own, you own it all!

Before the market crash of 2008, Capital One sent me a loan offer for $30,000 with a 2.99% interest rate for the first year and 1.99% for every year after. That was a ridiculously low rate. The small portfolio of homes I owned all had mortgages between 6-7%, which was considered good for investment properties. So 2% money was free money, as far as I was concerned.

I used Capital One's loan to buy a two-bedroom, 800-square-foot home in Oklahoma City proper. I paid $33,000 for it. $3,000 of my own money seemed like a reasonable risk to take.

The house had been totally rehabbed. I loved it. It was built in 1950 on cinder blocks, had a huge backyard, and was really cute. They called it a "military home". I moved a single mom and her young son in soon after closing.

After a few weeks of her living there, she called me and said "Greg, we have a problem. The plumbing is going in reverse. The things that are supposed to be going down are coming up." That's a paraphrase. She was much more explicit. But you get the idea. I had never heard about or seen anything like that. I went over to the house and sure enough, it was as she had said. It was nasty.

I immediately moved her and her son into a hotel because it was unsanitary to remain. I called my plumber Bob and explained the situation to him. He said he would bring out his auger and dig a hole in the backyard to access the pipe directly.

After being there an hour he called me and said "Greg, we have a problem." I was like "Bob, I know that, that's why you are there!" He replied "No, no, it's a much bigger problem. The pipe from the house to the main sewer line is compacted. We can't break through." You don't want to think about that too long. The only solution was to lay a whole new sewer pipe from the house to the city line. It was going to cost $7,000! Twenty percent of the entire house's value. OUCH.

REACH FOR RESPONSIBILITY

I said "Bob, you know what's funny about this situation? I never made any deposits to this line that contributed to the backed-upness and now I've gotta pay for 60 years of other people's crap I had nothing to do with!"

Isn't that how life works? Somebody else creates the problem and you and I get to fix it. This is where a lot of people bounce on the owner's mindset because "it's not fair." You're right, it's not. I used to tell my kids if they want "fair," they can go to the state fair during the first two weeks of September. That's the only place in life we're going to find fair. Once we settle that little issue, we're free to move on with our lives.

LIFE'S NOT FAIR

I literally had nothing to do with the compacted line, but since I owned the house, it was my responsibility. When I called the mom to tell her it was going to take a few more days, she said *"Greg, take all the time you need. We are eating waffles for breakfast every morning and swimming in a pool every night."* She didn't concern herself with the issue, the cost, or have any sympathy for me. Nor did she offer to help. Why would she? She didn't own the property. She was just renting.

At work it's difficult to take fully responsibility, especially when the crap-creator is just down the hall causing the issues you get to fix. It's frustrating. It's annoying. It's not fair.

Yet it's inherently what's required if we're going to bring an owner's mindset. This unlock is the one most people think of when it comes to "buying in." If you own something, anything, when it goes sideways, regardless of cause, you bear the responsibility to make it right.

IT'S ALL YOUR FAULT

One of the greatest benefits of an owner's mindset is that it encourages you to own it all. The compacted sewer line, metaphorically speaking, as well as the good stuff. As Michael Korda says, "Success on any major scale requires you to accept responsibility" (1977).

You may say, "This sounds like a *bad* thing, Greg. You had legal ownership of that house so you were responsible for what happened on the property. But why should I take responsibility at work beyond the expectations of my job?"

Taking responsibility for it all pays off in many ways. A study in *Current Research in Behavioral Sciences* found that individuals with a strong internal locus of control, meaning those who believe they are responsible for their own outcomes, are significantly more satisfied with their jobs and experience less stress at work (Padmanabhan 2021). Taking responsibility gives perspective, freedom, and truth. Taking responsibility counteracts the passion in our society for blaming others.

OUR LIFE IS A RESULT OF OUR CHOICES!

This includes, but is not limited to, our emotions, thoughts, feelings, money, time, relationships, successes, failures, skills, and so on. We've chosen this life, even if it doesn't feel like it.

We live in a blame-based-society, saying things like "You make me so mad." Or "My feelings got the best of me." Or "It's not my fault for going along with what they were doing." Every public scandal, the plea is "Not guilty." Even when you, I, and they know they are. Most plead not guilty in an attempt to avoid responsibility for the consequences of their actions.

The great fear of ownership is the cost of responsibility for the outcome. If we claim it at the beginning, we also carry it through to the end. Humans are wired to avoid loss. In *Thinking, Fast and Slow* (2011), Daniel Kahneman explains this clearly, "Loss aversion refers to the relative strength of two motives: we are driven more strongly to avoid losses than to achieve gains." When we sense even a small possibility of failure, or imagine looking bad in front of others, that threat outweighs the potential reward. As Kahneman also writes, "If you think in terms of major losses, you tend to be very risk averse." We don't resist ownership because we lack ambition. We resist it because our minds are trained to shrink back from the weight of obligation, the possibility of regret and the potential loss of reputation.

Work is interdependent. No one does anything in isolation. We don't bear all the burden and we don't get all the credit. Certainly it can seem like individuals do, but organizations are ecosystems connecting multiple people doing multiple things. Which is another reason folks fear ownership. We can't control what other people do or don't do.

Even if we do our best, someone else might negate those efforts, or even make them counterproductive. If we are successful, they may try to take credit for it.

WE CAN'T CONTROL OTHERS

This is what separates great leaders and managers from average ones. Great leaders take responsibility for everything. As President Truman's desk sign read, "The buck stops here." When a leader owns their role and their responsibility, they are much more effective at empowering and equipping others to do the same. When a leader resists an owner's mindset, they motivate with fear and toxic authority.

Remember Adam Neumann from WeWork? His fear-based leadership eventually destroyed morale and the company. Or they micromanage like our friend Melissa from Chapter 5. In contrast, leaders with an owner's mindset assume responsibility and offer support, trust and autonomy.

RESPONSIBILITY GIVES US A BETTER PERSPECTIVE

One of the things I've discovered sharing this content over the last decade is that everyone has a slightly different definition of what it means to "buy in." It's a phrase heard at work regularly when talking about getting people to rally around a project, direction, vision, or new effort.

There are definitely some challenges to "buying in." When we're asked to buy in to a new initiative, it is daunting because of the time required to invest in it. No one wants to be taken advantage of, so we're tempted to refrain from fully investing in the new initiative. We face a choice.

DO WE RESIST AND RESENT, OR RESPOND AND REACH?

In the early days, every time a tenant moved out of a home, I would begrudgingly clean it and get it ready for the next person.

I did this on Saturdays when there were plenty of others things I wanted to do. Also, I don't like cleaning. This combination created a cocktail of negativity in my mind before I even got to the home.

Most of the time, after I had been there a few hours, running to the store to get light bulbs, deep cleaning the bathrooms, vacuuming a couple of times, and overall getting it looking good again, I found myself in a happy mood. In the midst of the drudgery, I started feeling grateful that I was able to own this home and offer a space for families.

DON'T DRINK THE COCKTAIL OF NEGATIVITY

The work didn't change. My dislike for the work didn't change. Just my thinking did. As has been proven time and time again, and can be found in ancient literature to current self-help books, THE WAY WE THINK IS WHAT DEFINES OUR LIFE!

Instead of carrying anger and frustration about the new initiative, we can choose to reach for responsibility, embracing every aspect of our role in the organization. Having an owner's mindset is an ethos for expanding our lives, empowering our work, and unlocking a worthwhile future.

Remember Security Gate Steve from the Origin Story? Here is a guy who turned a literal "gatekeeper" job into a highly desirable and dignified position. It went from simply opening and closing a gate (yes, it was done manually every time) to being in a role that kept 800+ campers safe, creating security for students and parents alike. His personal reach transformed the role into something others wanted to be part of. Every job has meaning. Sometimes it takes someone reaching beyond their borders to reveal why a role is so important.

RESPONSIBILITY IS FREEDOM

Often individuals think having an owner's mindset only benefits the organization. They think it will cause them to sacrifice more of their personal life for their professional life.

I'd like to step outside of work for a moment and ask you to join me in considering how taking ownership of our entire lives benefits us. It's an odd ask, I know. Of course you own your life!

Maybe. I've found many who willingly rent out their mental, emotional, relational, and spiritual lives.

There are numerous memes that use the phrase "This moment lives rent-free in my mind" and then shows a memorable clip. That moment is not paying rent, you are… with your thoughts and focus, otherwise known as attention.

Of course the meme is a humorous indicator that whether serious, sad, shocking, or sublime an interaction can leave a mark on our mind. However, we pay for every second of attention we give it.

PAY ATTENTION

It costs us to fix our mind on something. I don't mean momentary thoughts that bubble up and disappear. I mean thoughts that we decide to take and make our own.

This takes us back to owning our lives. Whenever we are tempted to make excuses, justify our inaction, or blame others, we want to work to get back to the place where we can say "I am 100% responsible for every choice that has gotten me to this place in life." Whether or not this statement is literally true, embracing it enables us to see life, experiences, relationships, and opportunities quite differently.

Being 100% responsible weirdly gives us complete freedom. Until you've done it, it may feel like an extra burden. As if somehow you have to be responsible for other people's decisions, words, and actions. Not at all. We are not responsible for what they do. We are responsible for our *response* to them. We get to be responsible for our decisions, words, and actions. That's not unjust, is it?

REACH FOR RESPONSIBILITY

This mindset gives us a huge advantage. We are never the victim* if we adopt it. Oh, lots of unfair things can happen to us, sure. People can do us wrong. Others may take advantage of the situation ... but the power of an owner's mindset removes emotional hijacking, being manipulated, people-pleasing, and the compulsion to get even. Other people can't throw you off your game, because your game isn't about them. It's about 100% responsibility for yourself.

There is a lot of aspiration in our society for mental health and emotional well-being. An owner's mindset affords us contentment because we retain 100% responsibility. It's not a burden, it's an invitation to freedom.

When we react to the negative emotions of others, we rent out our soul to them. When we try to be responsible for their actions, we rent out our minds to them. If we let them own our well-being, we forfeit our autonomy and become dependent on them. Then we blame them for our internal upheaval. It's a vicious loop.

However, when we take the stand that we are 100% responsible for the entirety of our being, it creates an internal safe place for us. We can weather the storms of whatever other people are doing, because we are content with how we are living.

* In context of work and your choices.

TRUTH, LIES, AND AN OWNER'S MINDSET

I believe in ownership so fiercely because whenever we abdicate our agency to an external force, we lose part of ourselves. When we do that over and over and over, the victim mindset takes hold. When that happens we start practicing lie-based decision-making. We deceive ourselves into thinking or saying, "There's nothing I can do about it."

When our choices aren't based in truth, the consequences will be dissatisfying at best, disastrous at worst.

The ancient wisdom offered a couple thousand years ago still rings true and reminds us that truth sets us free! Over the course of history and in our lives, this proves accurate time and again.

Every time we blame someone else for our state of life, we propagate a lie and experience a loss. When it's someone else's fault, we can't own it. You and I can't control others, so placing responsibility on them removes our ability to change whatever is happening in us. It's a doomed loop of lies.

I've believed the lies in my own head. I've made decisions based on those lies, not recognizing my own self-deception, and it cost me dearly. From my first marriage, to my leadership role in the non-profit world, to parenting and being a professional speaker, I've absconded from responsibilities. I know what it's like to let insecurities dictate my actions, to feel sorry for myself, to justify my inaction, and to give up trying to alter my soul. We can further discuss the details one-on-one, if you'd like.

George Costanza famously said "Jerry, it's not a lie if you believe it." That's how a lot of society functions these days. The declarations of "My Truth" are smack against embracing an owner's mindset. We all have our own unique experiences in life that are true. That doesn't make them Truth.

When my kids were young they would say "You make me soooooooo mad" and I would reply "I don't make you anything." They didn't like that. When we shift and say "When you did this, I felt that," it keeps you and me responsible for our own emotions. When we outsource the responsibility for our emotional well-being to another human or situation, we risk our happiness. People do it all the time.

The resistance to the phrase "You Are 100% Responsible For You!" is saddening. People will immediately push back "But you don't know what my husband, wife, boss, sister, colleague parent, kid, friend, fill-in-the-blank, DID!!" It's THEIR fault I'm acting, feeling, behaving, thinking, responding this way.

I mean, I guess it keeps therapists in business.

Try this exercise. Fill in the blank for where you might be holding someone else responsible for your current state of emotions, financial life, mental health, physical, relational or spiritual well-being.

WHAT IF INSTEAD OF GIVING MY _____ THE RESPONSIBILITY FOR MY _____ WELL-BEING, WHAT WOULD IT LOOK LIKE IF I TOOK 100% RESPONSIBILITY? WHAT WOULD I DO? WHAT WOULD I FEEL? WHAT WOULD I THINK?

> We can run through many scenarios with those blanks.
> Parents ... Mental
> Spouse ... Financial
> Boss ... Emotional
> Work ... Physical
> Former spouse ... Mental, financial, emotional
> Past ... Emotional

That's a few examples. You can generate many more. Having a conversation with a friend or close colleague about where you place responsibility empowers you to shift it back to you.

The questions afterwards are more difficult when we don't believe in taking full responsibility. I can ask you to say it, however I am well aware that individuals will say it and then say

"But they ARE responsible for what they did to me." Yes, they are responsible for their actions, just like you and I are responsible for our actions.

Menlo Innovations, the tech firm in Michigan that emphasizes joy in the workplace, also models taking responsibility for it all. No one has private offices. Everyone works in pairs. Every decision is visible. Every failure is shared. When a project goes off track, there's no finger-pointing, just regrouping. Everyone is responsible for both the process and the product (Sheridan 2013).

I'm passionate about an owner's mindset because inherently it requires us to access truth, articulate emotions, accept reality, and act courageously.

THESE CREATE A SENSE OF FULFILLMENT, MEANING, AND PURPOSE IN OUR LIVES.

They're difficult, but satisfying. Hard, but empowering. Living 100% responsible for every area of our life feels a bit unfair, but it completely sets us free to live bold, passionate lives. It's also essential for the next aspect of an owner's mindset, Widening the Circle.

ACT LIKE AN OWNER

QUESTIONS FOR REFLECTION
- Where in my current role am I tempted to say "That's not my job"? What would it look like to reach instead of retreat?
- How could our team create a culture that celebrates taking responsibility, even when things go sideways?
- What's one area I've been blaming others that might actually need more ownership from me?
- How would my mindset shift if I viewed responsibility as a source of freedom rather than a burden?
- When have I taken full ownership of a tough situation? How did that grow my influence or self-respect?

CHAPTER 8
WIDEN THE CIRCLE

Once in a while, I would stop by the Brady Bunch house from Chapter 6. When I knocked on the door, the dad would answer and inevitably say "now's not a good time Greg." It never was a good time. He preferred to keep me out of the house. It was like a stiff-arm.

I would stand on the front porch thinking "Why are you treating me this way? I own this house. I'm providing a place for you and your family to live." It didn't hurt my feelings so much as confuse me. I'm the kind of person who likes to engage with individuals who have a direct impact on my life.

ACT LIKE AN OWNER

I realized I'd experienced the same behaviors at work from team members who worked in different departments. They would be gracious to one another, but not open to others. And if someone seemed to encroach upon their turf, they'd quickly find a way to escort them out.

Organizations are famous for having silos, self-contained departments that don't communicate or work well with each other. You can find the "us vs. them" mentality in businesses ranging from 10,000 people to ten people. Even scientists are not immune. Alfred Wegener proposed the theory of continental drift in 1912. He was not taken seriously by geologists because he was a meteorologist, and it wasn't until decades later that his theory was confirmed (Kuhn 2012). It took an outsider to the field to perceive an important truth. Unfortunately, the outsider was shunned for decades. He did not live to see his theory become orthodoxy.

Silos are a big problem for the ownership mindset. If you're going to bring your heart, head, and hands to your work, and you're investing in the organization as a whole, on occasion you'll certainly have ideas about how to do things beyond your department. Unfortunately, silos prevent this exchange.

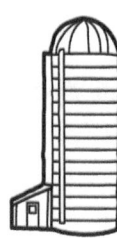

It took me a bit to figure out this dynamic, but once I

realized the cause, it enabled me to work on solutions to widen the circle.

People find their identity in their authority. Each of us has a sense of security because of our own unique expertise. When that feels diminished or threatened, our defenses kick in. Whether it's gained by education or years of developing expertise, our knowledge gives us a security in our strategies, decisions, and self-image. That is threatened when someone with neither expertise or education asserts themselves in our space.

Imagine if someone from your HR department dropped by the sales team meeting and said "Hey guys, we've been talking it over in HR and we have a few ideas that we think will really up your sales game."

After silence, laughter, or asking "who are you?," the sales team would shift to interrogation.

What do you know about sales?

When was the last time you sold something?

Do you even know anything about what we sell?

Do you have any experience or education in sales?

In this imaginary scenario, the best outcome is that the sales team would totally humiliate the person. The most likely outcome is they would disregard them and snicker after they left.

Here's another example from a different angle. What if someone from the frontline showed up at the executive leaders meeting and offered a suggestion about strategy? There might be an expression of gratitude, but they would be quickly dismissed because "you don't really understand what happens at this level."

Both the sales and executive responses would be true to life. You can play this scenario out among a variety of departments, divisions, verticals, locations, or service lines. Suggestions from another department will get the same basic response the dad gave me. A firm go-away-stiff-arm.

Think about it. When you tell someone from another department that their ideas are not welcome, you emphasize the renter's trait of skill (hands). The ONE attribute of a renter's mindset! If someone is thinking about your department (head) and cares enough to want to share it (heart), they possess an owner's mindset. The very thing we want!

Yet time and time again, organizations fail to design systems that support this kind of cross-functional interaction. Leaders claim to have an "open-door policy" that welcomes all guests. Unfortunately, the door has never been the problem. It's the openness of the person behind the door that matters.

Consider what happened when Target expanded into Canada.

The brand had everything going for it with capital, consumer demand, and market momentum. But internally, teams operated in silos. Merchandising moved faster than IT could support. Supply chain logistics  lagged behind product decisions. As a result, shelves stayed empty while warehouses overflowed. Within two years, Target Canada shuttered all 133 stores and wrote off billions, all because different teams couldn't work together (Dahlhoff 2015).

Let's imagine a different scenario. The Sales Team Leader regularly invites someone from HR to "sit in" on their weekly meeting. No pre-work is necessary. Just come and listen and at the end, the HR person is invited to share their perspective about what they've heard. Does their team have a similar challenge or have they solved similar problems, just in a different context? Can they bring an entirely different perspective? Building regular interdepartmental contact into the organizational structure widens the circle, enabling people to share and receive perspectives from other departments less defensively.

This happens daily at FastCap, a manufacturing company in Washington State. At FastCap, collaboration is built into the workflow. Everyone is trained in Lean thinking, and everyone is expected to contribute improvements. An ownership mindset is distributed throughout the team. One example is the shipping department noticed repeated delays because product specs didn't match the box labels. Instead of blaming the production crew, they worked side-by-side to redesign the packaging line. This resulted in no rework being required, faster fulfillment, and better margins (Akers 2014).

FOUR STRATEGIES TO WIDEN THE CIRCLE
STRATEGIC INVITATION

Strategic invitation is a strong solution for widening the circle. If we want our people to show up daily with an owner's mindset, the way we meet matters. Utilizing cross-functional teams, not just for accomplishing tasks, but sharing solutions, is vital.

Pixar's Braintrust is a prime example (Catmull 2008). Every morning during production, the team gathers for a ritual called "Dailies," where unfinished scenes are shown and discussed across departments. Lighting artists hear from story editors. Editors learn about rendering constraints. Everyone contributes and everyone learns. This rhythm of open feedback builds connection, deepens empathy across disciplines, and keeps ego in check. In short, it widens the circle. This practice has helped Pixar maintain high creative standards across films and departments without silos or ego-dominated turf wars.

Be mindful, however, because people's egos will be threatened. Imagine if someone from HR did create a sales breakthrough? In an ideal world, that's awesome. In reality, that's a hard pill to swallow for the sales team. Fostering an environment that prioritizes heart and head as well as hands will consistently produce the best results. To paraphrase Harry Truman, we can really kill it here if no one cares who gets credit.

STRATEGIC INVOLVEMENT

When the stove and oven from the Brady Bunch house needed replaced, I asked the mom to give me a list of five stoves and ovens she liked. Brands, colors, features, styles, etc. I ended up going with the second most expensive one. She was ecstatic! Not only did she love using them daily, she also was grateful for having a voice in the decision that was going to impact her life.

It's startling how leaders don't involve people who are going to be directly affected by a decision made. It's not always practical and some decisions aren't up for discussion. But in the world we're living now, if leaders aren't looking for ways to involve next-gen leaders who carry out the consequences of their decisions, they will lose these young people to organizations who do involve them (see Chapter 12).

Involvement doesn't obligate us to go with what the person wants, but it does communicate we're interested and open. That willingness goes a long way in connecting hearts and heads. It's not difficult to widen the circle. It requires a little imagination and a lot of curiosity.

Southwest Airlines involved frontline staff when designing uniforms and updating aircraft interiors (Shine 2017). They held design showcases and let employees vote and give feedback. The final designs reflected frontline needs, from functional pockets to flexible fabrics. This involvement didn't just result in better uniforms, it deepened pride and ownership throughout the ranks.

STRATEGIC INCENTIVE

Cross-collaboration is difficult to achieve consistently. Typically, when departments do that it's because one vertical (department, silo) needs the other vertical to provide something for them. They aren't incentivized to create a unique working arrangement between the two of them that works for both.

When rewards are embedded in the culture for different departments working together and finding new ways to succeed, it empowers teams to be more open to that kind of engagement. Microsoft under Satya Nadella redesigned performance incentives to reward collaboration across teams (Vander Ark

2018). Previously, departments competed for resources and recognition. Nadella shifted performance reviews to value collective wins and contributions to others' success. This incentivized engineers, product managers, and sales teams to work across divisions. That shift in how success was measured transformed Microsoft's culture and its market value.

STRATEGIC INTEGRATION

Uniting the head (imagination, critical thinking) and the heart (care, passion) doesn't show up on most strategic plans. Why not? It's the strategic integration of every strength in the organization. Businesses are arranged by the hands (skills, abilities) because that's how the work gets done. However, in the future, workplaces that don't integrate the heart and head of their employees will lose. Widen the circle or your results will shrink.

IDEO, the famed design firm, is structured for integration (Amabile, Fisher, and Pillemer 2014). Teams are intentionally cross-disciplinary, where a mechanical engineer works next to a psychologist who works next to a storyteller. Every project team integrates different ways of thinking so that creativity is maximized and blind spots are avoided. It's the business version of *no room exists without the rest of the house* (see the next chapter).

ACT LIKE AN OWNER

As long as there have been departments, there have been silos. Us vs. Them is rampant in every size of organization. It's easy to see why that is. However, we can be intentional about implementing strategies that widen the circle and bring more voices and ideas to the problems we face. Once and for all, let's bridge the gaps that are debilitating our forward progress.

QUESTIONS FOR REFLECTION
- Where do I see silos showing up in our organization, and how might I take the first step to bridge the gap?
- When have I stiff-armed someone with a fresh idea because they weren't from my department? What could I do differently next time?
- What simple rhythm or structure could we introduce that invites voices from outside our immediate team?
- Which cross-functional partnership could help us solve a current challenge faster or more creatively?
- What mindset shift is needed for me to value contribution over control when others step into my space with ideas?

CHAPTER 9
THINK WHOLE HOUSE

In 2007, I bought my all-time favorite home, a 2100 square foot, four-bedroom with the backyard against a greenbelt and two houses down from the neighborhood pool. Despite my past experience with the vandal college boys, I moved five Alpha Gamma Delta sorority sisters into it.

I loved the idea of having sisters rotate in and out every year. College girls are much cleaner than college boys, though that may be true of women and men at any stage of life. I offered to put an "ΑΓΔ" above the garage and make it an unofficial westside sorority house.

Three of the young women got their own rooms upstairs, while two shared the primary bedroom downstairs. It was a big room with an even bigger attached bathroom.

The young gal in the upstairs middle bedroom pinkified her room. It was like a color bomb exploded and turned everything pink. I'm a pretty easygoing landlord, so paint doesn't hurt my feelings. I liked people making their room their own so they loved living there and never wanted to leave. She also had a poster board overflowing with pictures of her and her boyfriend. Spring break trips, formal dances, picnics and so on ... young love captured in a shrine to him. When I entered the room I felt the necessity to bow down and recognize his presence in the room.

One time I stopped by and discovered that the ladies in the downstairs bedroom had put a hot iron on my carpet, not once, but twice. I was stunned. What in the world? How does something like that happen? It was new carpet too.

Do you know what the sister in the upstairs pink room thought about the iron marks on the floor of the downstair bedroom?

Drumroll please ...
ABSOLUTELY NOTHING!
It wasn't her room. She never went in it. What

happened there had no effect on her life. She didn't care.

She believed that her room was the most important room in the house. It's where she spent the majority of her time. It's where she did all her work. It was personalized to accommodate her. What happened in anyone else's room wasn't her concern.

This happens at work all the time. There are those who think their department is the most important one in the whole company. They say things like "If it wasn't for us, this whole place would fall apart." It's a limiting perspective that doesn't consider the whole house. But boy do they believe it's true!

A RENTER'S MINDSET SAYS MY ROLE IS MORE ESSENTIAL THAN ANYONE ELSE'S.

They sincerely believe it and have evidence confirming that what they do is critically important. They tend to think other rooms are fine, just not as significant.

Do you know someone like that?

That sentiment exists in small and large companies alike. But as the owner of the house, do you know what room I think is the most valuable?

You guessed it, each room is equally important. I like the

upstairs bathroom as much as the downstairs laundry room. I like the kitchen and all the bedrooms. They all serve a different

purpose, but are entirely interdependent on one another. A house full of bedrooms that doesn't have a bathroom wouldn't be worth much. And vice versa.

In reality, a room outside of the house has no value. It's a box in a field. What gives each room value is that they are part of the house. They're usefulness only exists in the context of the other rooms.

It's understandable that someone highly values their department or role. It's their hands, their area of education, experience, and expertise. Naturally, there is a bias. Think Whole House *is strictly heart and head.* It's completely an owner's mindset. It has nothing to do with skills, it's all about how we see ourselves in context of the whole.

When I speak to executives, the biggest ask I make is this. When you come to your leadership meeting, are you showing up as a representative of the room you lead? Or as a representative of the entire house, with responsibility for a specific room? It might sound like semantics. It's not.

In his book *The Five Dysfunctions of a Team* (2002), Patrick Lencioni says that each of the members of a team should be willing to subordinate their own parochial agendas for the good of the team as a whole. That kind of team health requires leaders who see beyond the walls of their own room. When leaders prioritize the house over their room, the whole house wins. When they don't, division seeps in and everyone feels it.

If a leader comes to the meeting simply to fight for their room's priorities, they do the organization, and their room, a disservice. After all, the room's whole purpose is to contribute to the house. If the leader comes to the meeting thinking about the whole house and understands how their room fits into that picture, they serve both the organization and their room well.

When there is dissonance in an organization, you only have to go up the leadership chain to find a person  who values their room more than the house. That's where the divisive trickle-down effect starts.

I'm not saying be a "yes man" or someone who automatically capitulates to other rooms. Take a stand. Lead with conviction. Voice your perspective and say what your room needs to succeed. Every room needs to be healthy, including your own.

Your level of whole house thinking is revealed when another room causes you pain. When an unexpected challenge occurs in another department (room) and requires assistance from you and your room, we quickly hear your heart. In healthy organizations, people may not love it, but they don't begrudge or speak negatively because if one room is failing, the whole house is.

If the upstairs bathroom starts leaking, it might not seem like any room's responsibility, but it impacts every room severely. If someone doesn't jump in quickly, the foundation could be impacted, the usefulness of other rooms affected, and the overall value of the house diminished. Caring about the whole, whether or not it has an immediate, direct impact on your room, is evidence of an owner's mindset.

How can we be intentional about keeping our perspective for the whole?

Doing so is even more challenging when you have locations in multiple cities, states, or countries. The scale of the organization combined with the demands placed on each individual makes it unlikely most will feel altruistic towards other departments and locations, especially if there is a problem. Most people think "Come on, I'm doing my part, I need you to do your part!" Most don't feel like they have extra margin to lend a hand to those in need.

THINK WHOLE HOUSE

COMMUNICATION IS THE BEST WAY TO KEEP THE HOUSE CONNECTED

If we want people to care about rooms they don't work in, we've got to give them access. And the best way to create access is through intentional communication. The further removed someone feels from a team, site, or decision, the easier it is to disconnect. So how do we keep hearts tied to the whole house?

Here are four communication strategies that enable people to think whole house.

1. CREATE SHARED EXPERIENCES
- Use town halls or company-wide gatherings to unify the house.

When the whole organization is brought together, whether monthly, quarterly, annually, in-person, or virtually, it reinforces that everyone belongs to something bigger. These aren't just update meetings. They're opportunities to connect people to purpose, spotlight cross-team wins, and remind every room that they're part of a house worth thinking and caring about. When done well, shared experiences aren't just informational, they're emotional glue.

2. VISION-CENTERED STORYTELLING
- Tell stories that spotlight wins from other departments.

We remember stories more than spreadsheets. Sharing real moments from across the organization, whether client successes, internal breakthroughs, or behind-the-scenes heroics, helps people see how their work fits into the big picture. These stories deepen emotional investment across rooms.

3. SHARED SCOREBOARDS
- Report progress in ways that reflect collective success.

When each team only hears about their own performance, it fuels siloed thinking. But when leaders communicate broader, shared metrics like customer satisfaction, culture health, innovation gains, etc., it shifts the narrative. Shared scoreboards invite everyone to take pride in the whole house, not just their section of it.

4. CUSTOMIZED CHECK-INS
- Adjust your communication based on the personality of each room.

Every room is different. Some need big-picture vision, others want tactical clarity. Some thrive with data, others with feelings. When leaders take time to learn how each team prefers to be communicated with and then adapt their approach, it fosters trust. And trust keeps hearts and heads connected to the house.

Maintaining an organization-wide ownership culture requires proactive communication at all levels. The "my room is the most important room" mentality that is so prevalent can be virtually eliminated with a consistent communication strategy that reflects an owner's mindset.

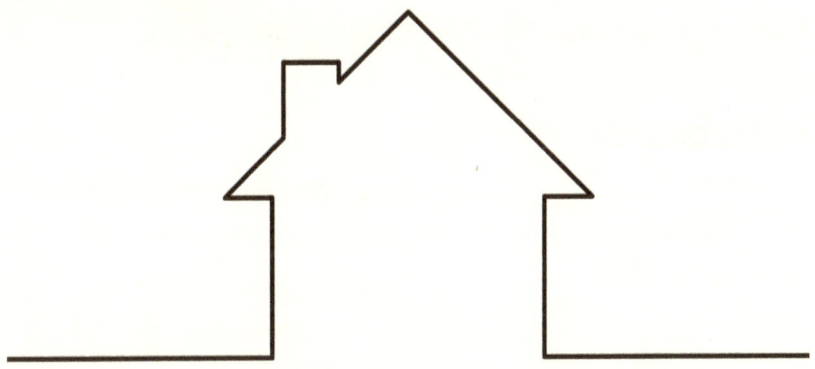

This final piece of the ownership puzzle puts everything together and allows everyone in the organization to be on the same team. As my client Mark Fisher of Alliant Insurance Services, formerly Advanced Benefits, says,

When our employees began seeing the bigger picture, they gained a sense of belonging to something greater than their day-to-day responsibilities. This shift has led them to adopt better decision-making habits, strengthen team morale, and create a

more profound impact on our clients and the greater community we serve.

Think Whole House is difficult because you have a full-time job to do in your room. You're in that room because you create the most value there. To care more broadly or think more critically requires an investment, an expansion of your skills and vision beyond your job description. *Is the investment worth it?* Chapter 11 concludes Part 2 by exploring this question.

QUESTIONS FOR REFLECTION
- Where am I currently more focused on protecting my room than serving the whole house? How might I reframe that?
- What happens in our organization when one room struggles? Do we respond like owners or like unaffected renters?
- What's one shared scoreboard or story we could spotlight that would help unify our team around a bigger mission?
- How do I currently show up to team or leadership meetings? Am I representing my department or the entire organization?
- What intentional communication practice could I start to help others feel more connected to the house, not just their room?

CHAPTER 10

YOUR LIFE IS AN INVESTMENT

I've asked you to consider fully embracing the Five Unlocks of an ownership mindset towards your organization.

RISK BOLD COMMITMENTS

Focus on *contributing* to your organization.

Take *accountability* with the help of a progress partner.

ACTIVATE LASTING VALUE

Create psychological safety for everyone to be candid.

Pay attention to your colleagues and find ways to recognize them with specific, thoughtful *free words*.

REACH FOR RESPONSIBILITY

Choose to be 100% responsible for the mission of your organization and your life.

Focus on finding solutions rather than blaming others.

WIDEN THE CIRCLE

Intentionally integrate with other departments, respecting their expertise while looking for ways to cross-collaborate.

Incorporate strategies to avoid silos in your organization and stifle Us vs. Them thinking.

THINK WHOLE HOUSE

Develop communication strategies that keep hearts and heads connected to the big picture vision.

Prioritize the house over the room.

You might be thinking, dang Greg that's asking A LOT. It is. Embracing these Unlocks will cost you. It requires energy, thoughtfulness, and courage. This is not the easy or comfortable path. It's the meaningful, purposeful path that satisfies.

Why should you take it on?

You are already going to work. Why not make it an investment instead of it being an expense? Lots of folks are spending their time, not investing it.

I'm rooting for you to invest. Invest in developing new skills. Invest in working with a progress partner. Invest in growing your expertise and confidence through strategic alliances. Invest in yourself by acting like an owner.

At this point, I often hear people say that all that sounds good in principle, but…

I JUST DON'T HAVE THE TIME.

Time can be your ally. Time is the great equalizer. We all get the same twenty-four hours. Throughout all of history, in the present and the future, everybody gets the exact same amount!

Time has all the makings of a best friend.

> He's **generous**. Waste him today, he still shows up tomorrow.
> He's **consistent**. Gives everyone the same twenty-four hours.
> He's **merciful**. Ends one day so another can begin.
> He's **kind**. Never holds a grudge.
> He's **reliable**. You and I will run out; he won't.

Too many people have an antagonistic relationship with time.

They say things like "I just need one more hour in the day." Or "I just wish there was another day in the week." Or they'll say things like "I ran out of time."

We humans are funny with hubris. We created a thing called "time management," as if time needed to be, or could be, managed. Time was here before us, time will be here after us. We don't manage time. We lead our lives in light of our relationship with time. I have personally decided to become good friends with time.

BECOME FRIENDS WITH TIME

We don't work with him, for him, or by him. We work in him. When you choose to appreciate the freedom you gain by accepting the twenty-four hour container he offers us to work within, it alters how you talk, think, utilize, and organize your day. You own it.

Do even a tiny bit every day, and it adds up. Behavioral economists refer to this as the *aggregation of marginal gains*. The idea that small actions, repeated consistently, compound into massive outcomes over time. In *Harvard Business Review*, Eben Harrell explains how 1% improvements over time led to gold for Britain's Olympic cycling team (2015).

James Clear, author of *Atomic Habits* (2018), echoes this by saying, "Every action you take is a vote for the type of person

YOUR LIFE IS AN INVESTMENT

you wish to become." The way you invest your time today, tomorrow, and the next day builds your legacy. Owners live with that awareness. Renters live for the weekend. Vandals live for themselves.

Understanding time causes you to think about your life as an investor and not a spender. An owner's mindset treats your time as an investment. A renting mindset treats your time as an expense. A vandal mindset eventually bankrupts you.

YOUR LIFE DESERVES YOUR INVESTMENT!

Do you know why I invested in properties? I wanted to gain a return on that investment through long-term equity, short-term rents, or preferably both. At work, when we invest, we want a return, too. Different people want different kinds of returns, but everybody wants something.

As a leader it's important to know what our direct reports are hoping to achieve. As an employee, it's important to be able to communicate the return we'd like.

Here's the framework I use with teams to identify motivation and desired returns. I call it **EFROG**.

EMOTIONAL

Some people see themselves as "go-to" people. Part of their identity lies in being someone who helps in times of crisis or who solves problems no one else can. Two different personality types, but the same desired return. The sense of fulfillment that comes to this individual floods their heart with positive emotions. It reinforces their sense of self and confirms their identity.

When this is someone's primary motivation, be mindful. They can turn bitter about others not willing to jump in and help. When this happens, they tend either not to say anything for long periods of time and eventually erupt, or carry quiet grudges that are uncharacteristic of who they naturally are.

FINANCIAL

Who doesn't want more money? Sure, it's not everyone's primary motivator. And even when someone says it is, you might find they value one of the other returns even more. But there are some people whose primary motivation for going beyond expectations is to be considered for a raise, bonus, or promotion. They want the bosses to see what a willing team player they are and to compensate them for their loyalty and work ethic.

RELATIONSHIP

Some folks want to be around others who are further along on the journey. They will work nights and weekends if it puts them in proximity of individuals they value. It could be their own colleagues, people in other departments, or leaders. These individuals live by the mantra "It's not what you know, it's WHO you know," and they'll make extra effort to know others and be known in return.

OPPORTUNITY

Some people are strategic in their career trajectory. These go-getters will exert themselves significantly for the possibility to exert themselves even more on a different challenge, account, or problem. They want you to see their capacity and give them a chance to do more with it. What some see as a painful problem, they see as an invitation to solve bigger problems in the future. They understand that "more work" could actually be the pathway to more significant work.

GROWTH

In contrast to our opportunity peeps, these individuals know that putting themselves in challenging situations will expand their capacities. They aren't looking for external progress per se, but internal growth. They are conscious of their own capabilities and want to get better.

This isn't the only way to grow, but it is an accelerated one. Working through a difficult scenario stretches us in ways nothing else quite does.

⌂

Knowing what motivates you and the people you work with is essential. We all can make our day an investment or an expense. If we invest, we would like a return on our investment. Knowing the kind of return people are looking for is critical to making their investment worth it. Of course, leaders are in an excellent position to create an environment where your desired return is achievable. But even if you're someone's co-worker, you can be mindful of the return they're looking for and support them.

What's liberating is, when we approach each day as an investor, regardless of what happens, we can find a win in it. It may be an educational return. It may be discovering a characteristic about a peer. It may be that an aspect of ourselves is revealed. We consciously act like an owner when we remember that we are the primary stakeholder in our life.

That's exactly what ikigai promotes (Garcia and Miralles

2017), a daily investment in purpose, meaning, and growth. In Japanese, "ikigai" means "a reason for living." Studies show people who cultivate ikigai report improved mental health, resilience, and even longer lifespans. When we view our day as an investment in things we love, things we're good at, and things the world needs, we start making intentional deposits toward a meaningful life, regardless of our title, role, or the day's events.

NO ONE KEEPS INVESTING WHEN THEY DON'T GET A RETURN

When we invest, we own. Yet many work environments don't offer up the necessary returns, so people who start out determined to invest as owners get converted to renters. Some even jump to being vandals because of their disappointment and frustration.

This reality is why I've gotten pushback over the years when talking to regular people about acting like an owner. I've heard numerous times and in numerous ways the phrase "*It's not worth it!*" It's not worth it to care. It's not worth it to go above and beyond. It's not worth it to remain loyal. It's not worth it to make the sacrifices. I get it. Often times it is not. However, any investment takes time to mature. If we pull out too soon, we'll never know what kind of return it would have paid out.

Over the last twenty years there have been several time periods where the headlines touted the advantages of renting over owning a home. They list the same standard reasons of cost, flexibility, ongoing or hidden expenses, and so on. Certainly, some homes are a money pit. However, the majority of houses persistently gain value and produce wealth for generations.

I'm not suggesting staying at one company for 30 years is the way to wealth, success, and satisfaction. However, the return on remaining in one place for an extended time does produce value that may not immediately be seen in a paycheck, but positions us for unseen returns.

.: NOTE to LEADERS :.

No one keeps investing if they don't get a return. You don't and neither will those under your care.

Just like quarterly dividends, there's got to be a visible manifestation of return on investment. Besides the paycheck, commission, and bonus, what is your organization offering? This conversation is necessary.

Sit down with those in your care and generate a dialogue to explore what would be meaningful and possible. Here are are few for your consideration.

RETURNS to CONSIDER

Aligned Purpose. Are you connecting the dots of an individual's sense of purpose with the organization's mission and business?

Ongoing Development. Are you equipping and enabling individuals to grow in ways that increase their value in the marketplace?

Open Mic Night. Are you consistently creating platforms where voices from all areas are heard and considered?

Curated Challenges. Are you supplying people the chance to tackle challenges that will enlarge their capacity even if it's in another service area?

Assigned Mentors. Are you giving experienced professionals the opportunity to invest in young leaders, while giving your less experienced employees the chance to partner with a mentor to accelerate their learning?

.: END NOTE :.

One thing for sure about Gen Z is that they value opportunities for advancement. Honestly, what generation doesn't? Gen Z is quite vocal about it. Social platforms expose them to how their peers are navigating the work landscape, including strategies to utilize for promotions. This knowledge amplifies their voices in the workplace.

From a company making a new hire to a leader spending her weekend on a client project, no investment is a sure bet. Sometimes investments pay off, sometimes they don't. We will never know what could have been, though, if we only rent our time at work.

Invest in your life daily and the odds are in your favor for some big returns over the course of your career, even if they don't show up where you expect. **Acting like an owner will always benefit you.** Here's a story from my editor Sam about a time he got an unexpected return.

As a relatively new faculty member at a very small liberal arts college, I was elected as chair of faculty senate during the first year of our new provost's appointment. Drawing on my father's expertise in organizational consulting, I introduced a number of innovations in the way that the college governance system worked. My passion was to have the voice of the faculty heard more effectively, and for the administration and faculty to be able to accomplish more together. I worked hard. To my surprise, by the end of the year I was appointed academic dean, which was not at all the outcome that I was expecting or pursuing at that early stage of my career.

YOUR LIFE IS AN INVESTMENT

QUESTIONS FOR REFLECTION
- Where am I currently spending my time like a renter instead of investing it like an owner? What would it take to shift that?
- What kind of return am I looking for in my work right now, whether emotional, financial, relational, opportunity, or growth? How clearly have I named that?
- How could I start treating time like a friend instead of a foe? What would that change about my workweek?
- When have I seen someone act like an investor and get an unexpected or long-term return? What can I learn from their mindset?
- What could our team or organization do to better reward ownership behaviors and sustain long-term investment?

PART 3
CREATING A CULTURE OF OWNERSHIP

CHAPTER 11
LEASE-PURCHASE OPTION

Look at you, you made it to PART 3! I really appreciate you sticking with it and continuing to read.

We have seen that organizations can be their own worst enemies. They can undermine their employees' initial enthusiasm to be owners and turn them into renters. In Part 3, we'll explore what to do when that happens. The good news is, change is possible. For example, when Uber faced a culture crisis in 2017, it wasn't the business model that was broken, it was the way people led. Under founder Travis Kalanick, internal investigations showed disrespect, harassment, and fear were common. Then, Dara Khosrowshahi arrived and took serious action (Mauri 2024). He introduced a clear code of conduct, leadership training, and mechanisms for whistleblowing and accountability. He led a new culture creation. Employee engagement surveys improved dramatically. Trust crept back into the system. And Uber transformed from a cautionary tale to a case study in ownership-based reform.

The resistance you feel about going all-in at your organization is because you doubt they will reciprocate. A feeling of one-sidedness hinders all of us because we don't want to be taken advantage of. As Sander van der Linden points out in *Foolproof* (2023), one of the most powerful barriers to belief and engagement is the fear of being made a sucker. People would rather withdraw than risk looking naive, which is why environments that prioritize transparency, fairness, and mutual respect are essential to sustaining an ownership culture.

Feeling like a sucker causes those initially willing to own their role to pause, step back, and recalibrate to a renter's mindset. This happens frequently. But what about when an organization genuinely decides to shape an environment that enables those who act like an owner to flourish? How do those organizations convince people who have already shifted to a renting mindset to go back to acting like an owner?

Offer a lease-purchase option. A lease-purchase option

LEASE-PURCHASE OPTION

gives both the company and the individual time to prove they are doing what they've committed to in good faith.

In real estate, a lease-purchase option creates a financial instrument that gives the tenant an on-ramp to convert their status as a renter into an owner. The simplest way to understand it is that the owner of the property becomes the bank. The renter makes a deposit, signs a contract, makes monthly payments, and assumes ownership responsibilities like insurance. Part of the monthly payment goes towards equity in the house. The difference between a lease-purchase option and a traditional mortgage is that the owner/bank puts a much shorter time-frame on when the property needs to be paid off. In other words, the renter/buyer needs to secure a conventional loan (or another financing arrangement) completed within the allotted timeframe, so the current owner/bank no longer holds the loan.

At work it's the same. There is a shared responsibility with the organization bearing the primary responsibility. It's up to leadership to maintain an ownership culture where transparency, trust, and candid communication are consistent.

In real estate this approach enables a person who can't currently secure a conventional loan the ability to start building equity and enter the path of home ownership. Both sides take a risk. The renter/buyer makes contributions towards the equity of the house without knowing whether they will eventually be able to finance the house. And the owner takes all of the usual risks of letting someone live in a building they are responsible for. Plus, they're giving up part of their long-term investment in the house's equity, since if all goes well, it will be purchased in the relatively near future.

At work the renter may not have the emotional or mental bandwidth to buy back in fully because they don't trust the leadership. Or they've had experiences where they feel they've been repeatedly treated unfairly. This option offers a gradual buy-back-in strategy.

As I've stated in Chapter 5,

MOST PEOPLE SHOW UP DAY ONE WITH AN OWNER'S MINDSET.

Only after being in a culture that squashes it out of them, proving there is no return on their investment, do they transform into renters or vandals (much to the disappointment of the leadership who, unfortunately are the ones who cultivated the renter/vandal culture in the first place).

LEASE-PURCHASE OPTION

For people in an organization who have already been pushed away from an ownership mindset, a lease-purchase option is needed to make it a reasonable and safe approach for them. It can feel risky. For an employee who has previously owned their role and then determined it's not worth it, the risk is with their heart and head. No one wants to play the fool. They already feel they went above and beyond, holding onto hope that the company would reward their efforts, but it didn't happen.

By shifting to an ownership culture, an organization is taking a risk, too.

- **Employee Autonomy**
- **Shared Responsibility**
- **Release of Control**

The autonomy afforded to employees to make decisions and spend their time in new ways can produce results or be a drain on resources. These don't seem like big risks, but it's why the majority of organizations don't foster this environment. It lessens control, and that feels extremely risky to leaders.

Even though both sides take a risk in the lease-purchase option, the organization must make the first move. They are the ones who nurtured the culture which prevented the employees from having an owner's mindset. They are the ones who betrayed the initial enthusiasm of the employees. When an organization says "We want you to buy in again," it needs to be backed up in three ways.

First, if leaders don't bring humility to the lease-purchase option, it's not going to get off the ground. This is best done wholesale. A town hall, company-wide gathering, or video confessional that offers something along the lines of, "We've failed you as leaders. We didn't cultivate a culture that enabled you to bring your best daily. We didn't respect your brilliance and autonomy …"

Okay, let's not get too carried away. If leadership simply acknowledges that their previous approach was less than stellar and now they've determined to go about it differently, that would be a win! An expression of desire for a new culture norm is actually a good starting point.

Without some sort of acknowledgement of past mistakes, it's a non-starter. Our egos won't let someone who feels they've been duped before be duped again. They would rather exert their energies outside of work or look for a place that facilitates their desire to own their role.

Second, the past breach of trust needs to be repaired. When a person starts a new job, they've entered into a contract that both sides agreed to. Because of power dynamics, namely who is

LEASE-PURCHASE OPTION

paying the salary, employees are the ones who face the immediate consequences of a renter/vandal culture. They are the ones who experience the hazing, who are forced out of their natural intention to own their roles, because they are worried they might lose their jobs if they don't conform to the culture. The company doesn't bear the consequences of enabling this culture until the employee pulls back, making little effort or even quiet quitting.

Creating a lease-purchase option is a rebuilding of trust, organization to individual, leader to teammate, colleague to colleague. That's no small feat, but possible if the organization makes a real commitment to transforming its culture and rewarding its workers' investments.

Third, there needs to be a full commitment among all leadership to engage in the lease-purchase process. If there isn't a full commitment, don't start the process. A partial attempt at creating a space for individuals to act like an owner will result in a backlash of painful proportions. Once you give yourself to the lease-purchase initiative, you must keep going.

.: NOTE to LEADERS :.

You've got to offer these...

HUMILITY • REPAIR TRUST • FULL COMMITMENT

When all of this is considered, the process of crafting a lease-purchase option offering is the almost spiritual act of re-engaging hearts and minds. Mindfully proceed in such a sacred undertaking. Remember,

Hearts = passion, energy, care

Heads = imagination, critical thinking, creativity

To find opportunities to re-engage someone, look for what caused them to disengage in the first place. If you hear "Nobody listened to what I had to say," find ways for them to contribute. "My work didn't matter," give them responsibilities they find more in alignment with their own values. "I felt isolated," expand their involvement across departments.

.: END NOTE :.

The problem is, sometimes leaders at all levels lie to themselves about their people, which makes this process harder. A leader might say something like "My people just don't want to work that hard." Bzzzz. Lie! People love to work hard if they find fulfillment in the work, are given effective parameters for succeeding, have good tools, are rewarded accordingly, and acknowledged for that work. It really is that simple. It's not easy. But it can be achieved by intentional design and communication.

What makes people enjoy their work?

Finding purpose in it. ♡😀👥

Utilizing their skills and knowledge. 😀👥

LEASE-PURCHASE OPTION

Enjoying their colleagues. ♡
Being stretched, but not broken. ♡🧠💪
Feeling and being valued. ♡🧠
Solving difficult problems that serves people.
♡🧠💪

Let's use the Five Unlocks of an owner's mindset as our guide for reengaging hearts and minds. Since leaders have to make the first move, the following is addressed to them.

Risk Bold Commitments

Why do you as a leader risk bold commitments? Why are you willing to take the risk? Hopefully by now you've defined your metrics of commitment and what it looks like for others to be committed in your organization.

How does your motivation for commitment translate to those renting? Would they be willing to take a risk if they believed, *like you believe*, that it's worth it?

We discussed how contribution and accountability are cornerstone principles of risk-taking commitments. Create an environment where you genuinely, and with interest, invite contribution from those with a renting mindset. Be willing to have meaningful conversation around their thoughts. When you offer a lease-purchase option, you may not even invite contribution about their own department. Enlist them to solve a problem in another department.

We think people don't want more work. We all already have tooooooooooo much to do. The reality is that when someone is invited to contribute in a way that gives them a return on their investment, they find the time and want to!

Connect people with progress partners who can help them grow. It seems counterintuitive because "who wants to be held accountable?" But when accountability programs are designed to increase people's skills and capacities, they appeal to anyone who wants to keep growing.

Activate Lasting Value

We spoke of free words and the potent power they possess when used with specificity. If you prioritize discovering and recognizing characteristics of those you are reengaging, using free words will make a big difference. You won't get far with manipulation or flattery. Insincerity will cost you.

Free words is one example. However, there are numerous other ways to make things better at your organization or community. Letting people participate in a way that generates real value to colleagues, clients, or the community will definitely connect their hearts and minds.

Gallup's meta-analysis consistently shows that when employees feel like their work matters, when they're seen, heard, and affirmed, engagement soars. One study showed that engaged employees result in 23% higher profitability, 18% higher productivity, and 43% lower turnover (Gallup Workplace n.d.).

Another significant way to activate lasting value is to invest in the person. Put them through a training of their choice. Give them access to knowledge resources. Be so bold as to send them to a conference. Or have it be as simple as an Audible account. **MAKE THE INVESTMENT** Making some sort of investment in them as a person and professional is hugely valuable!

Reach for Responsibility

Revisit EFROG in chapter 10. What makes them ribbit? If you don't know, start there. Once you find out, if and when possible, make sure they get that return.

It's incredibly powerful when an organization shifts its thinking from individuals to a comprehensive culture shift. Shaping an environment where everyone gets to contribute their best daily is the goal. An ownership culture creates a place where these opportunities are baked in.

When you think about aligning heart and head with tasks, consider their personal values. Not only do they want a return, they want meaning and fulfillment, which is embedded in the work we do. Help them extract it.

Widen the Circle

The collaborative nature of the world is evident. Watch any TikTok or reel and you'll see people doing them together. Listen to a podcast where often two or more are interacting. Go to a coffee shop and see two people body doubling to get work done. The world is one big collaboration! Next gen leaders think that's how work works. Even in isolation, they've formulated meaningful relationships through their gaming systems, social apps, and Venmo. I mean, even their banking involves friends!

If you aren't intentionally connecting high caliber people with one another, you are missing a big part of heart. People want to care about the work and they want to care about those they do it with. To reengage someone who is currently renting, introduce them to worlds they don't normally access. Systematize the open door!

Growing trust and building relationships transforms how we feel about our workplace.

LEASE-PURCHASE OPTION

Think Whole House

Ahhhh, there is nothing more satisfying than vision. One of the primary reasons a person moves into a renting mindset is because they lose sight of the big picture. Those closer to the top of the org chart tend to speak in terms of vision, direction, strategy, and anticipation. It's easy to remain connected to your heart and head because big picture possibilities generate excitement.

Incorporating whole house vision into conversations at every level is an ideal approach to wooing people back into an owner's mindset. When someone sees clearly how the room they're in and the role they play contributes directly to the mission, it is invigorating. Despite how big or small your organization is, it's shockingly easy to lose sight of how the day-to-day connects to the grandest, most important objectives.

⌂

This simple but powerful framework gives everyone a chance to buy back in, in a meaningful way, at a pace that makes sense, while watching leaders demonstrate their commitment to building an ownership culture.

A final aspect for creating a lease-purchase option is asking the leadership team to regularly discuss with their teams where they themselves rent sometimes. It's another act of humility that signals it's not an either-or proposition, that no one owns everything all the time, and that's okay.

When leaders reveal their own renting behavior and current specific areas of challenge, it creates an opportune space for others to discuss freely their struggles (remember the lesson from Cornbread Hustle's Cheri Garcia in Chapter 6?). Opening up meetings in an appropriate way to allow transparent conversations reduces the risk for renters to buy back in. Renters may be hesitating because they don't know if they can live up to it, so they'd rather not make a public commitment. However, if leaders willingly discuss their own dynamic approach to the friction between an owner's and renter's mindsets, it offers grace and freedom for others to also share openly. Frank conversations enable people to risk acting like an owner once again.

TRANSPARENCY ENABLES TRANSFORMATION

When the courageous decision to shape a culture for owners and invite renters to buy back in happens, true transformation is capable. For too long leaders have complained about disengaged employees, but haven't taken the responsibility to create a place they want to buy back into. Utilizing a lease-purchase strategy gives everyone a chance to make the process successful.

LEASE-PURCHASE OPTION

QUESTIONS FOR REFLECTION
- Where might I be acting like a renter, not because I'm unwilling but because I've been burned before? What would help me buy back in?
- How does my organization acknowledge past mistakes or rebuild trust after it's been broken? What would real humility look like in our setting?
- What's one thing I can do to re-engage someone on my team who has pulled back emotionally or mentally?
- Which of the five ownership Unlocks could help me create a lease-purchase moment for someone this week?
- If leadership created space for honest conversations about where people are renting, would I be willing to share? Why or why not?

CHAPTER 12
THE LOYALTY DILEMMA

The last decade saw the workplace go from a playground of toys, Nescafé, and twenty-four hour kitchens to being completely vacant. Since then, there have been multiple tests for what an effective office looks like, from remote to hybrid to in-office and every scenario in between. We are living in a time where there is no right way to do it. Every arrangement has pros and cons. Mix in different generational needs and it's a complex cornucopia of office roulette.

After graduating college at the University of Tulsa, my son Lincoln moved to Chicago for his first full-time job in 2022. They were fully remote. The initial consensus was that Gen Z loved remote because of the flexibility. However, what was true for my son was true for so many others who were desiring to advance in their chosen career. It's really hard to excel when you aren't around any seasoned employees, except on a screen. Lincoln is masterful at virtual relationship building, but there was no opportunity to shadow mentors or randomly engage in serendipitous conversations that would move him forward.

The result was an EFROG fail. Lincoln was not getting a sufficient return in this scenario. He left that job after the first year to go to a large agency that required three days in the office. He had an amazing direct supervisor who invested in him and advocated for him. She got to know him and created more opportunities for him to succeed. He was blossoming in every area as his desired ROI was being met. This is why understanding the EFROG of each person matters so much. Unfortunately, his amazing supervisor left and her replacement didn't fill the same role. Lincoln is a proactive guy and was well-connected to his colleagues and leaders. However, he was lacking the same personal attention. The replacement was several layers up in title, yet she and Lincoln split the workload. He started talking to management about a raise to compensate for the amount of new work he was taking on. They stalled, delayed, hemmed and hawed for months, so he started randomly applying for jobs.

Though he was consistent in articulating his feelings, they made excuses for why they couldn't give him a raise just yet. Granted most places aren't going to give a raise quickly just because someone asks. They loved his work and work ethic, but their structure didn't have the flexibility to accommodate his needs. So he took a job at a global corporation that gave him a 25% pay raise.

This company lost an employee who (dad-brag alert!) wrote the case-study submission for a campaign they did which won them the Grand Effie Award, the pinnacle of recognition in his field. Though his bosses would blame corporate structure for the delay, if they had really wanted to, they could have secured him a raise.

As a Gen X'er I struggle with this reality. When my son was communicating his professional frustration with his leaders, I encouraged him to keep it in perspective. He had a good job. He was doing work he liked. He was getting paid well. Like, chill out, dude. You've got a good thing going.

He possessed an owner's mindset. However, his loyalty and good-faith-commitment were not matched. The lack of reciprocity was too much for him to remain. It's not that he minded doing extra work. It's not that he minded waiting for a reasonable amount of time to be compensated. It's that when he kept giving and there was no sense of return, it crossed a line for him at some point.

LOYALTY STOPS WHEN SELF-BETRAYAL IS THE PRICE REQUIRED TO RETAIN IT.

That's the primary difference between our generations. My line was a lot further out. Gen Z's breaking point is much sooner because they've got data. They know the effect of moving jobs on gross income over time. They know the profits a company makes. They know the risks involved. They watch others do it on social media and see the results.

What's wild is that he wanted to stay loyal to the company. Yet they gave him too many reasons not to, primarily empty words and delayed acknowledgment. It's the same unfortunate scenario that plays out when leaders want their people to buy in, but turn them into renters.

The human spirit craves loyalty because it creates connection, fuels purpose, and literally lights up the reward centers of our brain. Loyalty isn't just a virtue, it's a hidden source of joy, meaning, and emotional resilience. It also affirms the kind of person we hope to be.

THE LOYALTY DILEMMA

Neuroscience research shows that loyalty is not just a noble ideal, but that it triggers a real, measurable reward response in the brain. Functional MRI studies have found that the ventral striatum, a key part of the brain's reward system, becomes highly active when individuals experience loyalty and social bonding (Daniel and Pollman 2014; see Zak 2017). In fact, the brain's response to loyal acts mirrors its reaction to tangible rewards like food or money. Can you believe that? It's like eating chocolate or finding a $20 bill in our coat pocket. Loyalty ignites all the good juju inside of us. What a sacred sensation!

As a species, we want to be loyal. Instead of proclaiming someone "disloyal" because they want to better their life, it may be more accurate to describe them as loyalty-deprived and looking to have that need met.

Give a Gen Z employee a sense of loyalty towards them and you'll get it back. This isn't anything we haven't heard before or seen in any national work survey. They want…

- Reasonable financial compensation
- Opportunities
- Expanded exposure
- To be invested in
- To be invited and included

Wait a second ... does that remind you of anything? I think these young leaders want their companies to buy into them. Whoa. Who knew that that kind of expression would result in deep loyalty? Hmm ... you and I knew, right?

The challenge, therefore, remains the same. How are loyalties aligned to work efforts and mission?

IT'S AS SIMPLE AND HARD AS CONNECTING A PERSON'S DREAMS TO WORK OUTCOMES.

The people who change the world are the ones who stay loyal to their own dreams and mission. If we're going to nurture loyalty in our organizations, it's going to be because employees at every level are afforded the opportunity to work congruently with their personal values and what matters most to them.

Granted, they also want to be compensated well. Who doesn't? You can't buy loyalty, but you can remove the distraction of feeling like they are falling behind on their earning potential.

My son would have happily stayed at his previous place if they had given him a 10% raise in a reasonable amount of time. He didn't need 25% more. Any amount that acknowledged his contributions would have been effective.

THE LOYALTY DILEMMA

Every generation has a bias hardwired towards loyalty. We all want the bullet-point items listed on the previous page. In his first job, Lincoln wasn't being invested in, invited, or included. In his second job, he wasn't getting reasonable financial compensation for his excellent and extra work. His investment was not reciprocated. If we can create a work environment, whether remote, hybrid, or in-person, that rewards loyalty, we will foster a legacy of teams and leaders with an owner's mindset.

> **LEARN THEIR EFROG ROI**

His story isn't unique. Across the business world, we've seen companies earn extraordinary loyalty simply by choosing to invest in their people at critical moments. During the 2008 financial crisis, software company SAS Institute made a bold move when CEO, Jim Goodnight, told employees that nobody would lose their job. That act of stability sparked emotional allegiance, which is a rare phenomenon. Employees worked harder, looked out for each other, and productivity rose despite economic uncertainty. Years later, SAS consistently ranks as one of the best places to work, not just for perks, but for its loyalty-first culture. Against a background of 17% to 25% turnover rates in the software industry, SAS has a turnover rate of 3% to 4% (Knowledge at Wharton 2011).

Loyalty matters, but it cannot develop in isolation. It needs a supportive environment to take root and grow. If we want loyalty to last, we must build a workplace where it makes sense to stay. That kind of place doesn't happen by accident. It has to be designed. That's where we're going next.

QUESTIONS FOR REFLECTION
- Where in my work experience has loyalty been rewarded and where has it been taken for granted? What lesson did I take from that?
- How clearly does our organization connect investment in people with long-term loyalty? What signals are we sending today?
- What am I doing to create a place where others feel safe to stay and motivated to give their best?
- When I feel the urge to leave, do I pause to ask if I'm loyalty-deprived or truly misaligned? What would help clarify that?
- If our team sat down and asked, "What would make loyalty feel worth it here?" what would we hear and what would we change?

CHAPTER 13
DESIGNING AN OWNERSHIP CULTURE

In any great home, design makes it feel cozy, peaceful, and welcoming. From the exterior to the interior, the layout of rooms, the choice of furniture, art, fragrance, and color, we sense a place immediately upon entering.

Work culture is similar, with the twist that design encompasses in-person, remote, multiple locations, and global outposts. Today when someone says "I'm working" they could be at a different desk than they were yesterday. They could be in their home office. They could be at a coffee shop, on a train, or in a hotel. That could be at a shared workspace or a different company building in a different city. They could come into the office three days a week or none at all. They could live many states away from the actual office building.

EVERY SINGLE VARIATION THAT EXISTS TODAY ENABLES AN OPPORTUNITY FOR THE EXPRESSION OF CULTURE.

One of my favorite examples of culture design is Menlo Innovations. Menlo wanted to build a better way of working (Sheridan 2013). From day one, co-founder Rich Sheridan made culture the centerpiece of their strategy. They forged it with clarity and intention. The team worked together to co-create their values through conversations focused on joy, collaboration, and transparency. This influenced the physical workspace with open-floor designs, the hiring process with paired interviews, and the daily rhythm of work with mob-style programming and visible whiteboards for progress tracking.

One of their guiding principles is "Make mistakes faster." This value gave employees the freedom to take action, experiment quickly, and learn without fear. Over time, Menlo earned a reputation for exceptional service and extremely low turnover. Visitors often refer to it as a "culture lab" they wish they could replicate. Menlo's success came from a decision to intentionally design a culture they wanted to work in and from.

I've had conversations with hundreds of people about how they define culture. It varies dramatically, with some common phrases that emerge as shorthand summaries such as "the way we do things here," "how the place feels," "what's tolerated," and "how we think and act."

Culture can be the byproduct of factors as disparate as the office setup, the founder's personality, the age of technology used, art on the wall, food in the break room, and the history of the organization. These factors combine in hard-to-predict ways. When I work with organizations who want to design their culture and not just leave it up to an amalgamation of chaotic chance-factors, I use a simple three-phase process.

1. DISCOVER VALUES

Every organization already has values. They are not something you make up. They are currently embedded in the beliefs, attitudes, communication, and actions of every employee, from the C-suite to the front line. Discovering these values involves exploring employees' experiences over the course of time, through collaboration and conversation. I love this initial phase. The interaction is raw, pure and eye-opening.

In Patrick Lencioni's book *The Advantage* (2012), he references four types of values.

Aspirational. These are the things we wish we were and hope to become. They're not quite true of us ... yet!

Permission-to-Play. These are ones like "respect," "integrity," and "honesty." We can't even function as an organization if these basic human needs aren't honored.

Accidental. These occur over time. They might say "our people are most important." But when it comes down to it, efficiency might actually be more important than any one person. Or someone may say "collaboration" is a core value, but when pressed, you might find "meeting a deadline" or "making quick decisions" are actually more accurate.

Core. These are the ones that are unearthed through the discovery process. They are foundational to who we are as a group of people.

Discovering our actual values helps us learn what is currently true about our organization and what needs to be altered. What we're aiming for is to eliminate accidental values. We want all of our values to be intentional choices, whether core, permission to play, or aspirational.

2. DEFINE CULTURE

What kind of place do we want? This is an imaginative exercise constrained by reality. Companies can't magically change themselves in sharp contrast to their current values. Too many employees have experienced false promises. For example, an organization may say "We are a place who values all voices." But in reality they only ever listen to a few. You can't instantly become the opposite of what you are.

INSTANT CULTURE CHANGE WON'T HAPPEN

We use words to fashion the space we're designing, but decisions and behaviors will always reveal if those words have potency. So in the process of changing culture and defining what we're aspiring to, it's vital that any tensions between aspiration and reality are publicly addressed.

3. DESCRIBE BEHAVIORS

How people act, respond, engage, resolve conflict, deal with failure, communicate, treat others, and solve problems reveals "the kind of people" who work and succeed in this culture.

There is no unique right way to work together. That's what makes each business a distinctive ecosystem. There's this invisible thing, culture, that takes form when individuals engage with other individuals. It's a creative experience mostly unnoticed by those generating it. Every employee contributes to the culture. It's never a passive experience either. Every single day what you bring to work, whether in-person or from a distance, affects the culture.

To see the step-by-step process for designing an ownership culture, a Case Study is available on page 179.

BUILDING AN OWNERSHIP CULTURE

DISCOVER VALUES   **DEFINE CULTURE**   **DESCRIBE BEHAVIORS**

PROXIMITY AND CULTURE

Culture isn't limited to a physical central location, though part of what makes the central office an ideal place to foster culture is the permanency of the space. The spirit of an organization is carried by each team member, some better than others. Some people are more bought in than others. Some are more curious than others. Some are more willing than others.

The challenge of remote and hybrid work is maintaining culture. It's hard to replicate virtually the serendipities that can happen in person. However, when we discover values, define culture, and describe behaviors, these activities aren't location-based. Articulating what they look and feel like from a distance is vitally important. Creating an addendum on your values, *"What these look like virtually,"* is an important step in the process of designing an ownership culture.

HubSpot under the leadership of Katie Burke is a great example (Sull and Sull 2024). With thousands of employees spread across multiple countries and time zones, their culture remains strong. Long before remote work became the norm, HubSpot codified their culture into a document called the "Culture Code." It clearly defines their values, things like transparency, autonomy, humility, and adaptability, and how those values show up in day-to-day behavior, whether someone is in the Boston office or working from a coffee shop in Boise.

One of their secrets is giving employees clarity and freedom at the same time. Expectations are explicit. Values are reinforced constantly through onboarding, team rituals, and digital communication norms. Their intranet, Slack channels, and manager toolkits all reflect a shared language and set of principles. Because their culture was built to live beyond buildings, they were fully ready for remote work during the pandemic, which then amplified their identity.

If culture is not clearly visible and articulated, figuring out how it transfers over fiber optics is difficult. What remote work has done is expose the lack of intentional culture design. Virtual work doesn't diminish culture, it reveals weak spots that already existed. As a matter of fact, when this three-phase process is done correctly, I've seen culture MAGNIFIED in a remote workforce.

VALUES LIVE FREE OF BUILDINGS.

OWNERSHIP CULTURE

The Five Unlocks of an owner's mindset mesh perfectly with the process of designing culture through defining values. That's because the Five Unlocks don't just belong to individuals. They are the raw materials of a powerful, transformative culture. When intentionally embedded into the design and rhythms of a workplace, these attributes shape how people show up, how teams function, and how the organization excels. They provide the foundation that creates a through-line.

Shaping the culture creates the landscape for different personalities, skills, ways of thinking and seeing the world to come together and function seamlessly. Sure there will be friction, tension and pressure, but it will produce diamonds.

DESIGNING AN OWNERSHIP CULTURE

Risk Bold Commitments

Ownership Culture starts with a readiness to risk commitment, not just from the top down, but from all directions. Leaders don't measure commitment by time spent at a desk, but by depth of contribution and alignment with the mission. In a culture of ownership, commitment is mutual. The organization commits to its people with clarity, trust, and investment. And in return, people commit to the organization with effort, loyalty, and pride. Every time someone steps up to contribute in a meaningful way with excellence, they're acting like an owner. Every time a company chooses long-term impact for its employees over short-term gain to the bottom-line, they're doing the same.

Activate Lasting Value

An ownership culture refuses to settle. It believes that value can be created by anyone, anywhere, any day. Whether through problem-solving, encouragement, or innovation, people in an ownership culture are empowered to activate lasting value, not just through their role, but through their presence. They see possibilities where others see problems. They speak life into their teammates. And they create momentum, not because they were told to, but because they've been equipped to.

ACT LIKE AN OWNER

CULTURE GETS BETTER WHEN EVERYONE INSIDE IT GETS BETTER.

Reach for Responsibility

In a culture of ownership, people don't say, "That's not my job." They ask, *"Where am I needed and what can I do?"* This isn't about overworking or heroic effort, it's about owning the outcomes. When people reach for responsibility, they fill the cracks instead of pointing them out. They fix messes even when they didn't cause them. And perhaps most importantly, they take 100% responsibility for their attitude, their impact, and their growth. An ownership culture fosters psychological safety and personal accountability because without these, responsibility feels like a threat instead of a privilege.

Widen the Circle

Ownership doesn't exist in isolation. It thrives in connection. A true ownership culture is built on alliances, across departments, titles, locations, generations, and backgrounds. People don't hoard ideas or defend turf. They share resources. They invite collaboration. They elevate others. Leaders model cross-functional thinking, and team members are encouraged to "open the door" not just symbolically but structurally. This

Unlock dissolves silos, builds bridges, and ensures that value travels across the entire organization. The circle of invitation and involvement gets wider and wider.

Think Whole House

Finally, ownership culture is always about more than just your space. It woos people to zoom out and act like an owner of the whole house. This perspective shows up in meetings, in hallway conversations, and in how decisions are made. Leaders advocate for what's best for the organization, not just their team. Team members look for how their work connects to the mission. People are celebrated not just for what they do, but for how they elevate the entire environment. This mindset makes culture cohesive, resilient, and inspiring.

USE THE FIVE UNLOCKS AS A BLUEPRINT TO DESIGN YOUR OWNERSHIP CULTURE

When these Five Unlocks are intentionally embedded into your values, behavioral expectations, and culture design, you don't just get higher engagement, you build a place where everyone wants to bring their best. You transform your culture from a backdrop to a catalyst. An ownership culture changes not just what people do, but who they become while doing it.

.: NOTE to LEADERS :.

The Unlocks of an ownership culture are not a one-size-fits-all blueprint. Different organizations with different histories and values can emphasize different aspects of ownership. For example, some of my clients use the word "ownership" or "commitment" as one of their core values. Others use contribution and thinking whole house as behaviors they expect from their team members. As you design an ownership culture for your organization, consider which attributes would best suit your mission, history and current reality. Then find your specific words, phrases, and colloquialisms that resonate.

Be careful not to put the end result of a value AS THE VALUE. Those traits go in the "behavior" section. Again, after the next chapter, you can see a detailed culture framework with specific words and categories, in the Case Study. And remember, if you want people to own their role, you need to involve them in the design process so they can.

.: END NOTE :.

DESIGNING AN OWNERSHIP CULTURE

QUESTIONS FOR REFLECTION
- What's one part of our current culture that feels accidental rather than intentional? What would it take to redesign it?
- Which of the five ownership Unlocks feels strongest in our organization right now? Which one needs more attention?
- How do our values show up in day-to-day behaviors and decisions? Where might there be a disconnect between what we say and what we do?
- If we had to describe our culture to a new hire without using buzzwords, what real examples would we give?
- What small decision could we make this week that would reinforce the kind of culture we're trying to build?

CHAPTER 14
CONCLUSION

I appreciate you making it all the way to the end. I'm going to use the conclusion not as a summary, but as one more chance to convey the importance of an owner's mindset.

You matter.

Your work matters.

How you work at your work matters.

Choosing to live life with an owner's mindset is a smart decision. Of course, I'm biased. I've lived decades with this philosophy. While in the short-term it may feel like you're getting taken advantage of, in the long run, the exponential benefit is substantial.

ACT LIKE AN OWNER

When you use a 30-year mortgage to buy a home almost all of your initial payments are interest. After one or two years, it feels like you aren't making any progress. Time persists, however. Both the value of the house and the value of your payment increases. The gradual application towards the principle in each payment is pennies and dollars. But just like all compounding, it eventually snowballs into significant growth.

Choosing to act like an owner best positions us for all the unexpected that life and work brings. Life and work are not against us, but it can feel like it. They are both neutral parties in our daily adventure. I love the phrase and philosophy that says *"life is happening FOR us."* How we navigate this adventure is up to us. Here's how we can choose to move forward.

1. Risk Bold Commitments
2. Activate Lasting Value
3. Reach for Responsibility
4. Widen the Circle
5. Think Whole House

Our capacity to engage work and life this way is only limited by our willingness, focus, and dedication. We can overcome our inherent loss aversion and give ourselves completely to investing in ourselves. That's one of the reasons I love the owner's

CONCLUSION

mindset. Even if I'm duped by another, I can choose to use that setback as an opportunity to grow. **I am never a victim because I have agency**.

Bringing this mindshift to our family, work, and life lets us enjoy reality. Whatever happens, we retain the ability to define the scenario in a way that eventually serves us.

- Owners bring their heart, head, and hands.
- Those renting only bring their hands.
- And the dang vandals are divisive and destructive.

Don't we want to apply the best parts of ourselves to the most important aspects of our life?

- Heart = passion, energy, care.
- Head = imagination, critical thinking, curiosity.
- Hand = skill, ability, expertise.

There is so much emphasis on mental health and well-being both in life and at work. Do you think if an owner's mindset supports passion, energy, and care, that it might create a sense of belonging and well-being?

Do you think if an organization used the Five Unlocks as the blueprint for designing their culture, the results might be striking? Imagine if every day you "go to work," your heart and head are as deeply engaged as your hands. It's possible. Own it!

QUESTIONS FOR REFLECTION
- Of the Five Unlocks, which one comes most naturally to you? Which one will require the most intention moving forward?
- Where in your life or work are you still renting, and what small shift could move you closer to ownership?
- What would it look like for your heart, head, and hands to show up together more often? Where is one place to start?
- How can your team or organization use this book as a blueprint to shape culture, not just behaviors, but beliefs and mindsets?
- If you fully embraced the owner's mindset, how might your story change over the next year?

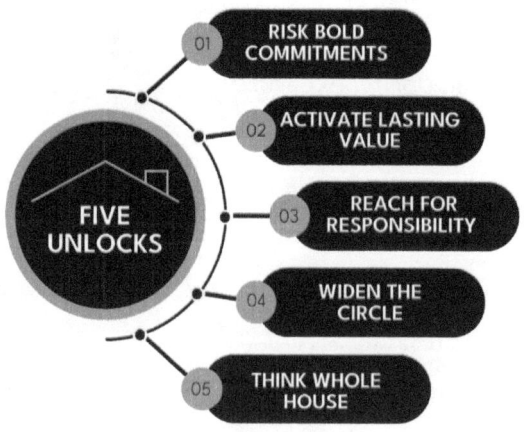

BEYOND THE BOOK

CASE STUDY
BIBLIOGRAPHY
ACKNOWLEDGMENTS
PERSONAL NOTE
ABOUT THE AUTHOR

CASE STUDY
A 10-YEAR CULTURE JOURNEY

The Regional Food Bank of Oklahoma was established on May 15th, 1980, one year after founder Rodney Bivens formed a task force to fight hunger. His own personal experience with food insecurity as a young person fueled his determination to make a difference.

He and the Food Bank became a force of good in Oklahoma County, then spreading out to serve 53 counties. The first year in existence, they distributed 280,000 pounds of food. In 2024 they distributed 16 million pounds of food!

32 years after Rodney established this incredible organization, he decided it was time to retire. He himself was a

force to be reckoned with, yet retained a humility and compassion that was ever-present. As he looked to retirement, he concluded that instead of having a statue built for posterity, that he would rather get intentional about shaping a culture at the Food Bank. That's the legacy he wanted to leave behind to the 120+ employees who had joined him on his mission to Fight Hunger, Feed Hope!

They had a diverse workforce including Donor Development, Community Outreach, Marketing, Administration, and the biggest department, Warehouse and Distribution. All of them worked in the same building. On top of that, they hosted volunteers every week from a variety of corporations, churches, community groups, and individuals. Thousands of people every year contributed to the preparing and packing of food.

The clients they served were equally varied, from Mom-and-Pop food shelters in rural Oklahoma to pantries in the metro area. In 2012, the Regional Food Bank launched their own Food Resource Centers because Rodney wanted to set a standard of getting the end user an experience of intentional dignity. It was as innovative as it was controversial. It seemed like he was "competing" with the very outreach depots he served.

This is when I entered the picture. They had never done any work specifically for their culture. They had a mission. They had

CASE STUDY

a vision. Everyone knew it. Most believed it. As a nonprofit organization, the majority of people who work there were moved by the mission. But not everyone. And it is a workplace. The challenges that for-profits face exist in the nonprofit world as well.

We launched a seven-month journey with the executive team. I met with them twice a month and we had lots of robust conversations. We became "One Team," built a playbook, defined communication strategies, and cultivated an enormous amount of trust. In the midst of that we ventured into values. This was more difficult than anyone imagined.

I also formed what I called the *Square Root Group*, with at least one member from every department. Most departments had more than one representative. It numbered about 12 people selected from a pool of those whom the leadership thought would thrive in the organization and lead it forward.

My conversations with the SRG initially focused on values. I brought them together on two different occasions to brainstorm and debate words and ideas with the One Team. After we landed on the values, we moved on to what those values looked like in real time. Both the SRG and One Team deliberated the details separately and collectively. We were all together when we signed off on the final version.

ACT LIKE AN OWNER

At the end of the seven months we held an organization-wide meeting to introduce the culture, values, and behaviors. At the time no one really could know what the impact would be. But we did everything possible to saturate the place visually and integrate the language into every gathering.

- Icons were created.
- Desk cards with reminders were placed everywhere.
- Posters were hung.
- The values found their way into interview questions.
- Annual reviews contained culture terminology.
- Praise and rewards were focused on values and behaviors.
- Values language was integrated into every team meeting.
- Conversations were casually had about their importance.

From the launch, there was a complete commitment and belief that this environment would spur on the next generation of leaders and employees.

On that page over there (and the next) are the three values we landed on. Every single word matters in the descriptor and listed behaviors. It's essential to describe both what the behaviors are and are not. CLARITY OF EXPECTATIONS gives everyone the same chance to succeed.

CASE STUDY

Expecting to be better tomorrow than we are today...

Core Value: VITALITY -- the force that drives us forward with energy and enthusiasm.

Core Value Defined	Demonstrated Behaviors
Vitality is... 1. Having a positive attitude and believing in one team, one goal and one mission. 2. Holding ourselves to the highest standards. 3. Being passionate and enthusiastic about what we do and who we serve. 4. Being willing to laugh and find humor in everyday activities. 5. Anticipating and embracing change. 6. Having physical and intellectual agility, vigor and energy.	• Demonstrates cooperation, teamwork and a 'can do' attitude. • Looks for the best in all people and all situations. • Consistently contributes ideas and solutions and actively participates in discussions. • Looks for ways in which to perform better and more efficiently. • Represents the organization in a positive light. • Assumes a leadership role when possible. • Encourages and promotes camaraderie among staff. • Believes that mistakes are learning opportunities. • Gives and listens to constructive criticism. • Remains flexible. • Creates opportunities for information sharing and inclusivity. • Takes ownership of work and supports others to do the same. • Self-motivated and confident.

Opposite of Value: *Avoids assuming responsibility; unsupportive of others; refuses to accept change; works against progress; exhibits a bad attitude; makes excuses; speaks negatively about the organization, its employees and policies; gossips; is complacent; creates drama; lacks enthusiasm and passion.*

Expecting to be better tomorrow than we are today...

Core Value: INNOVATION -- the spirit that drives us to pursue and initiate creative solutions.

Core Value Defined	Demonstrated Behaviors
Innovation is... 1. Proactively finding better ways to serve. 2. Encouraging creative solutions through collaboration. 3. Approaching challenges and unmet needs with a fresh perspective and purposeful thinking. 4. Using knowledge, experience, and intuition to make things better. 5. Thinking ahead - building for the future. 6. Willingness to take calculated risks.	• Displays desire and willingness to try new things and adapt to a changing environment. • Displays an inner drive and self-motivation in the search for new and better ways to accomplish objectives. • Collaborates with partners and colleagues in brainstorming activities in order to develop new solutions and processes. • Leads and encourages others to be creative and collaborative in solving difficult challenges. • Implements solutions, based upon calculated risks, which advance the mission. • Maintains a sense of optimism and determination in overcoming obstacles. • Leads the food banking industry in best practices. • Develops and shares new strategies to accomplish objectives. • Deliberately applies information, imagination, intuition and initiative to derive greater value. • Participates in strategy meetings and actively engages in discussion; empowering critical thinking and questioning. • Maintains a safe environment where calculated risks are used as learning opportunities. • Accepts that failure is an opportunity to learn and improve.

Opposite of the Value: *Fears trying something new; does things the same way just because they've always been done that way; automatically finds fault with new ideas; unwilling to think 'outside the box'; unwilling to listen to others; fears failure; being afraid to voice your point of view.*

ACT LIKE AN OWNER

	Expecting to be better tomorrow than we are today...	
	Core Value: **STEWARDSHIP** -- the commitment that drives us to care for the mission and resources.	
Core Value Defined		**Demonstrated Behaviors**
Stewardship is... 1. Framing decisions and actions around our core mission. 2. Using resources wisely, efficiently, and for their intended purpose. 3. Providing consistent dependability -- always doing what we say we will do. 4. Nurturing the relationships with those who help us carry out our mission. 5. Recognizing our moral obligation to the people and communities we serve. 6. Maximizing, investing, and putting to good use, our assets.		• Ensures a safe and healthy environment. • Leads by example, putting the needs of others first and helping people develop and perform to the best of their ability. • Cares for the environment and organizational assets. • Respects and safeguards the integrity and credibility of the organization. • Holds themselves and others to the highest standards. • Communicates clearly, providing follow up and follow through on all commitments. • Shows concern and respect for the time, beliefs, culture and experiences of others. • Builds trust by communicating with gratitude, transparency and integrity. • Relates to others and shows compassion without judgment. • Works to understand expectations and alternate points of view and behaves in a way that is deserving of trust. • Recognizes the importance of self-care. • Forms partnerships to compound the benefits and use of resources.
Opposite of the Value: Acts in self-interest; is careless or misuses resources; not responsive; withholds information; lies; displays a superior attitude; close-minded; values tasks above relationships; reluctant to participate in organization-wide activities; puts department needs and goals above those of the organization; takes others for granted; seeks credit and/or recognition for work done.		

There is A LOT packed into those images and words. These handy cards lived with team members.

What made this process so relevant and impactful was that it was not a "top-down" process. The leaders didn't get in a room in one day and determine what the values of the organization are. THAT NEVER WORKS. If there's a hint of insincerity, like "that's not really what we value here," rolling them out creates negative momentum.

Not only did every department have a voice in the creation, they each became **ambassadors who advocated for the values and culture**. These ambassadors would tell the story of how we landed on these words and ideas. So even when there was pushback, it wasn't leadership explaining, it was a colleague

CASE STUDY

offering their account about the rigorous process. Don't underestimate how significant and valuable it is to have teammates tell other teammates how the sausage was made.

THE PROCESS IS WHAT MAKES IT CREDIBLE!

Without the process, these kinds of endeavors won't be integrated into the reality of the workforce. They'll become static reminders of hollow aspirations that never materialized.

Rodney stuck around for another year, because, well, it was hard for him to leave his life's work, and the process to find his replacement was difficult. Eventually Katie Fitzgerald was selected to be the new CEO. She is an amazing leader who brought a new level of discipline and transparency to the operation. She also leaned heavily into the culture. She pressure-tested the values with new hires and old leaders. They became her filter for evaluating mission-moving projects and every major decision.

She graciously invited me to remain in the loop. I continued to contribute to executive meetings and all-staff events. It was quite a joy to see how Rodney's wishes for the culture to be his legacy took even deeper roots after he exited.

Three plus years later, Katie was drafted to be second-incommand at Feeding America. She currently serves as the CEO for Ronald McDonald House Charities, a global operation impacting hundreds of thousands of families. I'm honored that she still invites me to contribute to her teams about trust, values, and culture.

When Katie left there was a vacancy for over a year during COVID. Then Stacy Dykstra came onboard as the Regional Food Bank's CEO. She has a completely different personality from Katie or Rodney. Yet she too found usefulness in the culture and values. Her style of leadership is incredibly collaborative. As an empowering leader, she has high expectations because of that freedom and autonomy she's entrusted her leaders with. They own their role which creates enormous personal agency.

Once again, I was invited to collaborate with her and the executive leadership team. Though none of them were present for the original culture design, they all believed in the values and their impact on how people showed up to work.

Since a decade had passed, we decided it was time for a Culture Refresh. With a new generation of leaders and team members we realized language had changed and even what mattered had adjusted. It was a sincere look in the organizational mirror to ask "Do these still matter? If not, what does and how

CASE STUDY

how can we articulate it?"

The process time was cut in half, but the same model was utilized. We spent less time on the executive team coming together and more time focused on evaluating the words, ideas, and behaviors that defined the Food Bank as an organization.

Believe it or not there were one or two members who were in the original Square Root Group who were in this one too. Which verified they DID possess the qualities that would cause them to thrive, succeed, and make a difference in their work.

After a decade, only one of the three values remained, and we added one more. There was lots and lots of slightly combative, but always respectful, conversations about which words and ideas actually reflected truth and reality. No one shied away from expressing their opinion. Everyone involved knew how important the values had been up to that point and took seriously the task of framing the culture for the next decade.

Not only did we discover updated values, we also communicated them in an updated fashion. On the next few pages are the conclusion of that work.

ACT LIKE AN OWNER

*With courage, we demonstrate **HEART** by*
approaching our mission with compassion, grit and commitment.

*With courage, we demonstrate **STEWARDSHIP** by*
responsibly and efficiently utilizing the resources entrusted to us.

*With courage, we demonstrate **EMPOWERMENT** by*
advocating for equitable opportunities that elevate others.

*With courage, we demonstrate **COLLABORATION** by*
prioritizing teamwork as we listen, support and compromise to achieve our mission.

CASE STUDY

HEART *is*

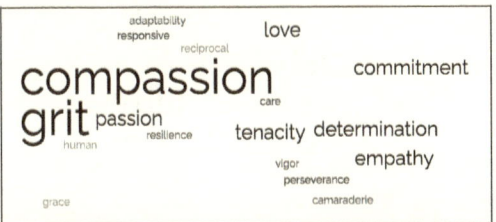

EMPOWERMENT *is*

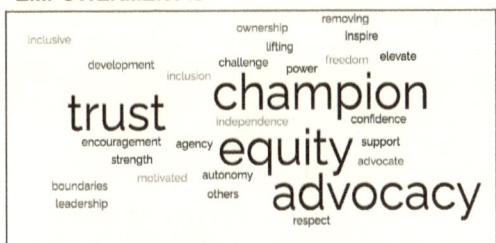

STEWARDSHIP *is*

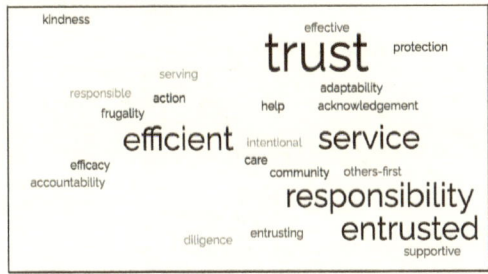

COLLABORATION *is*

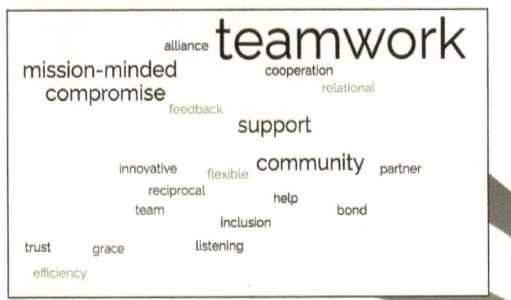

ACT LIKE AN OWNER

HEART *isn't*

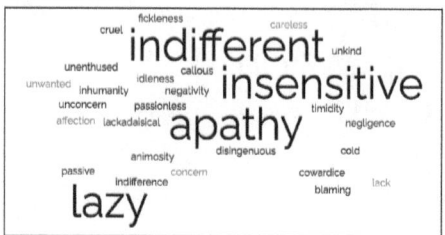

EMPOWERMENT *isn't*

STEWARDSHIP *isn't*

COLLABORATION *isn't*

CASE STUDY

Once again, we brought the entire staff together for a rollout. Another generation of employees who feel like the place they're investing their life in has values that align with them personally.

The value of values is immeasurable, though Gallup and others try to measure them all the time with...

- Engagement, leadership, retention and attraction
- Innovation and market share
- Awards and client feedback
- Productivity and safety
- The list goes on...

Discovering Values, Defining Culture, and Describing Behaviors elevates workplaces! When you shape it around an owner's culture, it enables people to act like an owner at every level of the organization. And who doesn't want that?

If you'd like to utilize the forty question ownership assessment to discover owner/renter/vandal levels in your culture, please scan the QR code.

BIBLIOGRAPHY

Akers, Paul A. 2014. 2 Second Lean: How to Grow People and Build a Fun Lean Culture at Work & at Home. 3rd ed. FastCap Press.

Amabile, Teresa M., Colin M. Fisher, and Julianna Pillemer. 2014. "IDEO's Culture of Helping." Harvard Business Review, January-February. https://hbr.org/2014/01/ideos-culture-of-helping

Amabile, Teresa M., and Steven J. Kramer. 2011. "The Power of Small Wins." Harvard Business Review, May. https://hbr.org/2011/05/the-power-of-small-wins

Campbell, Dakin. 2023. "The Definitive Account of How WeWork Went from a $47 Billion Valuation to a Basket Case in Just 6 Weeks." Business Insider, November 2. https://www.businessinsider.com/weworks-nightmare-ipo

Catmull, Ed. 2008. "How Pixar Fosters Collective Creativity." Harvard Business Review, September. https://hbr.org/2008/09/how-pixar-fosters-collective-creativity

Chapman, Bob and Raj Sisodia. 2015. Everybody Matters: The Extraordinary Power of Caring for Your People Like Family. Portfolio.

City of Denver. n.d. "Denver Peak Academy." Accessed July 15, 2025. https://www.denvergov.org/Government/Agencies-Departments-Offices/Agencies-Departments-Offices-Directory/Department-of-Finance/Our-Divisions/Budget-and-Management-Office/Denver-Peak

Clear, James. 2018. Atomic Habits: An Easy & Proven Way to Build Good Habits & Break Bad Ones. Avery.

Dahlhoff, Denise. 2015. "Why Target's Canadian Expansion Failed." Harvard Business Review, January 20. https://hbr.org/2015/01/why-targets-canadian-expansion-failed

Daniel, Reka and Stefan Pollman. 2014. "A Universal Role of the Ventral Striatum in Reward-Based Learning: Evidence from Human Studies." Neurobiol Learn Mem 114: 90–100. https://doi.org/10.1016/j.nlm.2014.05.002

Edmondson, Amy C. 2018. The Fearless Organization: Creating Psychological Safety in the Workplace for Learning, Innovation, and Growth. Wiley.

BIBLIOGRAPHY

Fisher, Mike. 2024. "The Brilliant Jerk vs. Team Performance." Fish Food for Thought, November 2. https://mikefisher.substack.com/p/the-brilliant-jerk-vs-team-performance

Fleck, Caroline. 2025. Validation: How the Skill Set That Revolutionized Psychology Will Transform Your Relationships, Increase Your Influence, and Change Your Life. Avery.

Gallup. 2023. Global Workplace Report.

Gallup Workplace. n.d. "What Is Employee Engagement, and How Do You Improve It?" Accessed August 7, 2025. https://www.gallup.com/workplace/285674/improve-employee-engagement-workplace.aspx#ite-691667

García, Héctor, and Francesc Miralles. 2017. Ikigai: The Japanese Secret to a Long and Happy Life. Penguin Life.

Gladwell, Malcolm. 2024. Revenge of the Tipping Point. Little, Brown and Company.

Hamel, Gary. 2007. The Future of Management. Harvard Business Review Press.

—. 2011. "First, Let's Fire All the Managers." Harvard Business Review, December. https://hbr.org/2011/12/first-lets-fire-all-the-managers

Harrell, Eben. 2015. "How 1% Performance Improvements Led to Olympic Gold." Harvard Business Review, October 30. https://hbr.org/2015/10/how-1-performance-improvements-led-to-olympic-gold

Heath, Chip and Dan Heath. 2007. Made to Stick: Why Some Ideas Survive and Others Die. Random House.

Housman, Michael and Dylan Minor. 2015. "Toxic Workers." Harvard Business School Working Paper 16-057. https://www.hbs.edu/ris/Publication%20Files/16-057_d45c0b4f-fa19-49de-8f1b-4b12fe054fea.pdf

Kahneman, Daniel. 2011. Thinking, Fast and Slow. Farrar, Straus and Giroux.

Knowledge at Wharton. 2011. "SAS Institute CEO Jim Goodnight on Building Strong Companies—and a More Competitive U.S. Workforce." Knowledge at Wharton Podcast, January 5. https://knowledge.wharton.upenn.edu/podcast/knowledge-at-wharton-podcast/sas-institute-ceo-jim-goodnight-on-building-strong-companies-and-a-more-competitive-u-s-workforce/

Korda, Michael. 1977. Success! How Every Man and Woman Can Achieve It. Random House.

BIBLIOGRAPHY

Kuhn, Thomas. 2012. The Structure of Scientific Revolutions. 4th ed. University of Chicago Press.

Lencioni, Patrick M. 2002. The Five Dysfunctions of a Team: A Leadership Fable. 20th Anniversary Ed. Jossey-Bass.—. 2012. The Advantage: Why Organizational Health Trumps Everything Else in Business. Jossey-Bass.

Littlefield, Christopher. 2022. "A Better Way to Recognize Your Employees." Harvard Business Review, October 25. https://hbr.org/2022/10/a-better-way-to-recognize-your-employees

Mauri, Terence. 2024. The Upside of Disruption: The Path to Leading and Thriving in the Unknown. Wiley.

Morgan, Jacob. 2014. The Future of Work: Attract New Talent, Build Better Leaders, and Create a Competitive Organization. Wiley.

Padmanabhan, Sindu. 2021. "The Impact of Locus of Control on Workplace Stress and Job Satisfaction: A Pilot Study on Private-Sector Employees." Current Research in Behavioral Sciences 2. https://doi.org/10.1016/j.crbeha.2021.100026

Pink, Dan. 2011. Drive: The Surprising Truth About What Motivates Us. Riverhead Books.

Robison, Peter. 2021. Flying Blind: The 737 MAX Tragedy and the Fall of Boeing. Doubleday.

Seligman, Martin E. P. 1975. Helplessness: On Depression, Development, and Death. W. H. Freeman & Co Ltd.

Sheridan, Richard. 2013. Joy, Inc.: How We Built a Workplace People Love. Portfolio.

Shine, Conor. 2017. "Now Arriving: Southwest Airlines Debuts Its First Uniform Redesign in 20 Years." The Dallas Morning News, June 19. https://www.dallasnews.com/business/local-companies/2017/06/19/now-arriving-southwest-airlines-debuts-it-first-uniform-redesign-in-20-years/

Sinek, Simon. 2014. Leaders Eat Last: Why Some Teams Pull Together and Others Don't. Portfolio.

Sull, Donald and Charles Sull. 2024. "How to Walk the Talk on Culture: Former HubSpot SPO Katie Burke." MIT Sloan Management Review, October 30. https://sloanreview.mit.edu/article/how-to-walk-the-talk-on-culture-former-hubspot-cpo-katie-burke/

BIBLIOGRAPHY

Vander Ark, Tom. 2018. "Hit Refresh: How a Growth Mindset Tripled Microsoft's Value." Forbes, April 18. https://www.forbes.com/sites/tomvanderark/2018/04/18/hit-refresh-how-a-growth-mindset-culture-tripled-microsofts-value/

Van der Linden, Sander. 2023. Foolproof: Why Misinformation Infects Our Minds and How to Build Immunity. W. W. Norton & Company.

Zak, Paul J. 2017. "The Neuroscience of Trust." Harvard Business Review, January-February. https://hbr.org/2017/01/the-neuroscience-of-trust

Zenger, Jack. 2025. "Discretionary Effort: 7 Leadership Levers That Drive Performance." Forbes, April 4. https://www.forbes.com/sites/jackzenger/2025/04/03/discretionary-effort-7-leadership-levers-that-drive-performance/

HAWKS MEDIA

ACKNOWLEDGMENTS

I am deeply grateful to the many people who helped bring this book to life!

To **Sam Ruhmkorff**, whose editorial insight sharpened every chapter, thank you for guiding the format and flow, pulling this out of my brain, and making sure it all made sense.

To **Monica Sheri Scott**, whose creativity shaped the look and feel of this book inside and out, thank you for bringing style, insight and excellence to every page.

To the dedicated group of beta readers who offered time, perspective, and honest feedback. **Michelle Hawks, Erin Greilick, Monica Sheri Scott, Regina Lane, Jack Myrick, David Burkus, David McLaughlin, John Bobb-Semple, Randy Nail, and Tom Hawks** this book is WAY better because of you. Your suggestions enabled it to take a giant leap forward.

To the **clients** and **audiences** who welcome me into your workplaces and conferences. Thank you for listening, implementing, and putting these principles to the test, and then sharing your feedback. I value our relationship.

To my professional speaking friends and non-speaking friends, thank you for cheering me on while you also change the world in your own ways. I learn from you every time we share a stage or a conversation. I'm super grateful for our relationship!

PERSONAL NOTE

I am profoundly grateful for the people and purpose that have shaped my life. At the core of it all is my calling. *To be useful in meaningful ways that provoke others toward greatness. Steward God's Dream.*

I am especially thankful for my *Life Advisory Board*: **Randy Nail, David McLaughlin, Steve Cunningham, Marty Loberg, and Rodney & Shannon Fouts**. Your wisdom, counsel, and endurance listening have guided me through countless decisions.

Joe Fronko, you've listened more than anyone. I'm grateful for all the years and miles.

My faith frames the highest calling of ownership as stewardship. I believe each of us embodies a unique dream of God, and our lives are an opportunity to discover and live it. I've been entrusted with this ownership message.

Lincoln & Lainey, I'm proud and enamored by how you own your lives in such powerful, fun, and amazing ways.

To my fabulous wife **Michelle**, what a ride! Thank you for consistently walking (and running) beside me. Your love, devotion, and smile strengthen my soul and sustain my spirit.

I aspire to live out the Five Unlocks. This book is one expression of that pursuit.

I invite you to pursue unlocking ownership, as well.

ABOUT THE AUTHOR

Greg Hawks is a keynote speaker, author, and consultant who challenges leaders and teams to **Act Like an Owner**. For more than 25 years, he has worked with organizations nationwide to build cultures of trust, ownership, and growth.

Known for vivid metaphors, dynamic energy, and practical insights, he delivers experiences that spark change long after the event ends.

This book is the blueprint. Greg collaborates with organizations to integrate its principles into daily rhythms so ownership becomes the culture.

When Greg isn't on stage or with clients, you'll find him running, camping under the stars, or enjoying life in Minneapolis with his incredible wife, Michelle. His two kids, Lincoln and Lainey, are the joy of his soul. He also delights in his bonus kids, Madeline, Carter, and Charlotte.

If you want the principles in this book alive in your workplace, email Greg. Whether speaking or consulting, he will empower your leaders and teams to shape an environment where everyone contributes their best daily.

hello@greghawks.com
www.greghawks.com